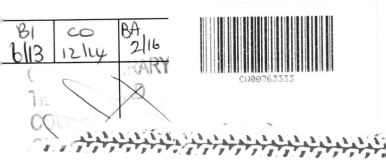

*Enjoying the top-notch singletrack of the Dunnerdale Fells*

# Lake District
# MOUNTAIN BIKE
# ROUTES

## 22 classic loops
## in the Cumbrian fells and dales

www.lakedistrictmountainbikeroutes.co.uk

# TOM HUTTON

**OTG**
**Out There** Guides

First published in April 2013 by
**Out There** Guides Ltd,
22 Crosland Terrace, Helsby, Frodsham,
Cheshire WA6 9LY.

Telephone: 01928 723744

Layout and design by Carl Rogers

Text and photographs © Tom Hutton 2013

ISBN: 978-0-957364-50-9

**Advice to readers and users of this guide**

*Whilst every effort has been made to ensure that the information in this book is correct, the author or the publisher can accept no responsibility for errors, loss or injury however caused. Check all details before you proceed. Your use of this book indicates your assumption of the risks involved in mountain biking and is an acknowledgement of your own sole responsibility for your safety.*

# CONTENTS

# INTRODUCTION

The Lake District is home to some of the best 'natural' mountain biking in the UK: an incredibly varied selection of tracks and trails that thread their way through some of the finest mountain scenery anywhere in the world. But finding these trails isn't always easy: a trail on the map doesn't always equal one on the ground; and even when it does, there's no promising that trail will be ride-able.

That's where a book like this comes into its own; highlighting not only the best of what's available but also suggesting tried and tested ways to combine them to make logical loops. Some of the routes are well-established classics and should be seen as rites of passage for all British mtb'ers; others are a little more esoteric: ideal for riders with a more pioneering spirit or just to escape the crowds on busy bank holiday weekends.

Some are short: a couple of hours at the most; and just right for bad weather days or a quick blast that'll fit in around other things; but there are also a few full day epics that require stamina and determination to keep going as well as skill. And while a few are technically easy and perfect for those making their first forays off road; there is plenty of full-on technical stuff included too.

In short, there's something here for mtb'ers of all abilities and all levels of fitness.

They are without a doubt some of the best routes I've ridden in 15 years of route research. I just hope that you enjoy them too.

**Tom Hutton** April 2013

*Singletrack in the Lickle Valley, Dunnerdale Fells*

# THE ROUTES AT A GLANCE

## Grizedale & Windermere

| | | | | |
|---|---|---|---|---|
| 1. | Hawkshead & Grizedale East | 16.5km/10 miles | Medium | 30 |
| 2. | Grizedale & Low Parkamoor | 27km/17 miles | Hard | 36 |
| 3. | West of Windermere | 13km/8 miles | Easy | 42 |

## Staveley & Kentmere Fells

| | | | | |
|---|---|---|---|---|
| 4. | The Garburn Pass | 18km/12 miles | Medium | 46 |
| 5. | The Green Quarter | 22km/13 miles | Medium | 50 |
| 6. | The Nan Bield Pass | 39km/22 miles | Epic | 54 |

## Ambleside & The Langdales

| | | | | |
|---|---|---|---|---|
| 7. | Loughrigg & The Langdales | 25km/16 miles | Hard | 60 |
| 8. | Loughrigg Fell & Loughrigg Terrace | 10km/6 miles | Easy | 66 |
| 9. | Hodge Close | 20km/12 miles | Medium | 70 |

## Coniston Area

| | | | | |
|---|---|---|---|---|
| 10. | Dunnerdale Fells | 14km/9 miles | Medium | 74 |
| 11. | Walna Scar Road | 21km/12.5 miles | Hard | 78 |
| 12. | Blawith Common | 19km/12 miles | Easy | 84 |
| 13. | Round Conniston | 32km/20 miles | Hard | 88 |

## Western Esoteria

| | | | | |
|---|---|---|---|---|
| 14. | Black Combe | 14km/9 miles | Easy | 93 |
| 15. | Eskdale | 19km/12 miles | Easy | 97 |

## Ullswater & the Central Fells

| | | | | |
|---|---|---|---|---|
| 16. | Helvellyn | 26km/16 miles | Hard | 102 |
| 17. | High Street | 35km/22 miles | Epic | 108 |
| 18. | Ullswater/Boredale Hause | 20km/12 miles | Medium | 114 |

## Howgill Fells

| | | | | |
|---|---|---|---|---|
| 19. | The Howgill Fells | 52km/31 miles | Epic | 117 |

## Around Keswick

| | | | | |
|---|---|---|---|---|
| 20. | Borrowdale Classic | 28km/18 miles | Hard | 125 |
| 21. | Back 'o Skiddaw | 32km/20 miles | Hard | 130 |
| 22. | Lonscale Fell | 17km/10 miles | Easy | 136 |

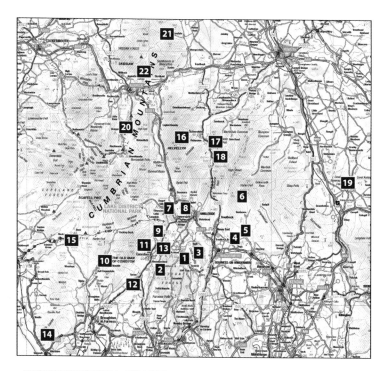

# WHAT THE ICONS MEAN

**Big Ups & Downs**
Huge climbs that could take well over an hour, and equally big descents

**Navigation**
Some tricky route finding where a map and compass or GPS may be useful

**Bad Weather**
A ride for all conditions—good on a bad day

**Technical**
Sustained sections of technical riding requiring good bike handling skills and some walking

**Push or Carry**
Expect to push or carry your bike on some sections

**Dry Only**
Delicate surfaces that are easily damaged when wet

**Mountain**
Climbs into the high mountains where bad weather could be serious

**Undulating**
Rolling hills rather than big ups and big downs

**Singletrack**
Plenty of narrow stuff for maximum fun

# HOW TO USE THIS BOOK

The idea of this book is not only to describe some of the best riding the UK has to offer, but also to make it as easy as possible for you, the reader, to choose the right route every time you go out. It's laid out in an arbitrary geographic order: from South East to North, making it easy to decide where to base yourself or to choose the routes that are closest to your base.

All the key ride information is displayed on the opening page of each ride so that at a quick glance you can see the grade (see opposite), length, severity of the ride and the time it's likely to take you. A series of graphic icons (see previous page) also offers information about the kind of riding the route contains and the kind of conditions you're likely to encounter. This should make it very simple to decide if a route is right for your ability, the time you have available and even the conditions on the day.

Next up, the **In Brief** section offers a little more detail; hopefully whetting the appetite enough to get you checking those tyre pressures and lubing your cables. The maps show the actual trails plotted on 1:50,000 Ordnance Survey mapping. The written route descriptions will talk you through any major decision-making along the way; but where possible, it's probably best to transpose the actual line of the route onto a GPS or map (or print out-of one) and then carry the book in your pack just in case you need to refer to it.

For those with limited time to enjoy all the mountain biking the area offers,

*Singletrack on Green Quarter*

we have compiled a **TOP FIVE** which are the routes that just have to be ticked. And for riders with a penchant for a particular type of riding, we've also awarded a stamp for the route with the **BEST SINGLETRACK**, the **BEST CLIMB** and the **BEST DESCENT**. But all the routes are top-notch so hopefully you'll return again and again until you've ridden the lot.

## A WORD ON GRADES

The grades **Easy**, **Medium**, **Hard** and **Epic** are of course subjective and fairly arbitrary. They are designed to take into account both the distance covered, the amount of ascent and the type of riding you'll find along the way. This is why there are some routes graded Hard that are very short and others graded Easy that are actually quite long. If it's a short Hard, it's going to include some serious going; if it's a long Easy, expect a cruise. More than half the routes are graded as Medium or Hard as this is the level where most mountain bikers operate. Epics of course speak for themselves: they are very long—usually the best part of a day—and pretty tough too; only fit, experienced riders need apply.

It's worth remembering that all the rides will get tougher if it's wet or windy.

## A WORD ON HEIGHT GAIN

It's not rocket science: the more height gain there is in a ride, the harder it's likely to be. And used in relation to the distance of a ride, it can also give an idea of how 'steep' a ride is e.g. a 600m height gain in a 20km ride is likely to mean more of the ride spent going up or down than a 600m height gain in a 30km ride. But interestingly, height gain doesn't have anything like the same effect on ride times as it does for walkers; basically because walkers descend at almost the same pace as they climb—say 3kph up and 4.5kph down, whereas a bike may slow to 3kph on the way up but may then descend at 20kph, or even 30kph. See below for more information on calculating how long a ride will take.

## A WORD ON TIMES

Times can be even more arbitrary than grades but those quoted are aimed at mountain bikers tackling distances they are used to on terrain they are

*It's important to eat regularly to keep energy levels up. Here Steph enjoys a quick snack*

*An old style GPS can make navigation much slicker*

*Sheltered riverside riding in Eskdale*

reasonably comfortable with. A really strong climber could possibly half some of them; and likewise a nervous newbie that doesn't enjoy rocky singletrack could add hours to some of the more technical routes if they were out of their depth.

A good way to estimate time is to constantly record your moving average speed while you ride, either with a GPS or computer, and you'll probably quickly arrive at a reasonably good moving average—on this kind of going it won't be a long way away from 10kph. Once you've arrived at this, simply divide the distance by the average e.g. 30km @ 10kph = 3 hours and then add a little, say 20mins per hour for stops to navigate, eat, mend flats or take photos. If there's any chance of darkness getting the better of you, it's worth leaving another hour for emergencies—it's difficult getting off the hill in the dark and an unplanned night will be no fun.

If you're at all unsure, start on shorter routes and work up to the harder/longer ones.

*Woodwork and signage on the manmade North Face Trail in Grizedale Forest*

## TAKING TO THE MOUNTAINS

Mountain biking has changed significantly in the last decade. The prolific spread of trail centres across the UK has led to a whole generation of fit and very able mountain bikers that have scant experience of riding in real mountains. Hopefully this guide will help them make that leap: and the next few pages will provide plenty of useful information.

It may also prove useful to riders more used to suburban or lower-level riding.

## WHERE TO RIDE

Every attempt has been made to ensure that all the routes featured in this book utilise trails that mountain bikes have a legal right to ride. They are predominantly bridleways and byways (including restricted byways), but also include public roads and other tracks often referred to as green lanes, which are actually un-surfaced public roads. These are shown differently on different scales and makes of map so it's worth checking the key on the actual map you are using to see how they are depicted.

# RULES OF THE TRAIL

Today's riders will shape the trails of the future, as well as the image of mountain biking. The following code has been produced by International Mountain Bike Association (IMBA UK) to encourage mtb'ers to enjoy their ride responsibly, while showing respect for others and care for the environment.

## 1. Keep It Legal

You can ride on bridleways, byways and restricted byways.

On Forestry Commission land you can ride on forest roads, except in the New Forest, where you need to follow local guidance. You can also ride any singletrack which is promoted for mountain bikes.

You can use some canal towpaths: check out the Waterscape website. You can also ride on designated cycle routes.

Scotland has its own access legislation and you can ride in most locations providing you do so responsibly. Obviously this falls outside the scope of this book.

## 2. Leave No Trace

Think about how you ride and the impact this has on the trail. Practice to improve your skill at low-impact cycling.

*Signage is good on most of the routes*

*Rampage by name, responsible by nature. Always ride with respect for the trails*

LAKE DISTRICT

*Erosion exacerbated by mountain bike tyres—the wrong route on the wrong day*

Wet and muddy trails are more vulnerable to damage. So adjust your riding and consider using alternative trails where appropriate.

Keep to existing trails; avoid widening the trail or creating new lines.

Always take your litter home with you. And other peoples' too if you can— inner tubes and cycle litter reflect badly on all riders.

*Firm surfaces and shelter from trees: Eskdale is perfect for those typical Lakes bad weather days*

### 3. Control Your Bike

Stay focused; even a second's inattention can cause problems for you and other trail users.

Check your speed. Ride responsibly, and think about when the conditions are right for riding fast. This awareness will avoid incidents with others.

Remember, there are inherent risks associated with mountain biking. Be realistic about your riding ability. Where appropriate, trail grading colour codes will give you an idea of what to expect from each trail.

### 4. Always Give Way

Let your fellow trail users know you're coming. A friendly "hello" or bell ring, is considerate and alerts others to your presence.

Pass slow and wide, slowing to a walking pace or stopping if necessary. This is particularly important when approaching or passing horse riders.

Saying "thank you", if other trail users give way to you is polite and helps build good relationships with others.

When approaching corners or blind spots, anticipate other trail users.

## 5. Avoid Disturbing Animals

Animals can be startled by an unannounced approach, a sudden movement or a loud noise. This can upset dogs, startle horses, scatter cattle and sheep or disturb wildlife. Be aware of your potential impact on animals and take care to avoid disturbing them.

## 6. Always Plan Ahead

Know your bike, your equipment, your ability, and the area in which you're going to ride and prepare accordingly.

Be self-sufficient. Keep your equipment in good order and carry necessary supplies for trailside repairs, and any changes in the weather.

Wear appropriate safety gear for the trails you're riding.

# THE BIKE

With a few exceptions you'll need a 'proper' mountain bike to ride and enjoy the routes described in this book. A tough fully rigid bike will cope—it's

*Sunshine and singletrack on Blawith Common*

*The author's trusty Ghost*

what we used to ride before suspension; but it won't be very comfortable and may not be much fun. A hardtail is always a good compromise and will be perfect on all but the most technical loops featured. Full suspension will generally make cornering easier and the steepest and most technical descents a little more ride-able but they tend to make climbing tougher. X-country, trail or all mountain type bikes will be best with only the most determined wanting to push a downhill rig up some of these climbs.

## KIT

### Helmet

These days helmets are pretty much de-rigeur for mountain biking and definitely advisable for the riding in this book, if not all cycling. Make and model is less important than fit but make sure it's adjusted correctly so won't move about in a crash.

### Clothing

Padded shorts are almost as essential as a helmet, although it doesn't really matter whether they are liners beneath baggy shorts, integral within baggy shorts, or, if you really must, just plain lycra cycling shorts. For your top half, layers are definitely the way to go, with a wicking base layer (short or long sleeved depending upon preference and conditions) as the foundation and then a choice of a top layers including a windshirt, which will make a huge difference without being too sweaty; a waterproof, which'll keep rain out but if you're working hard you'll get wet from the inside; and/or an insulation layer such as a fleece if the weather is seriously cold. Cycling style soft shell jackets are a blend of insulation and windproofness and a good choice for winter.

Remember to always have a spare layer with you; a bad fall or big mechanical could mean a lot of waiting around and you'll cool down very quickly in the mountains if you're not moving.

## Footwear

There's so much choice here. Do you go for SPDs (clipless pedals) or flats? If you choose the former, it limits you to footwear that will take a cleat

*Helmet and glasses*

*Baggies for those that don't have the figure...*

*Fingered and fingerless gloves*

*Wet and muddy trail shoes*

although these days the range of shoes available varies from full-on racing style (not recommended in the mountains) to full-leather walking style boots, which are great in the winter but heavy and a bit over the top on hot summer days. If you only have one pair then a pair of trail style shoes (like trainers) will be most versatile. Go for some with recessed cleats if possible; they'll grip a lot better if you're carrying/pushing on wet rock. A pair of overshoes will help in the winter.

If you prefer flats, the sky is your limit. Perhaps trainer style shoes for the summer and a pair of softish, lightweight walking boots for the winter?

## Gloves

Essential—everybody reaches out with their hands when they fall off. For normal riding it's down to personal preference: fingerless are cooler in summer, fingers are warmer. In the depths of winter you'll probably ditch your riding gloves in favour of some fleecy ones anyway.

## Eyewear

There's more to eyewear than looking cool: mud or a fly can really hurt and I daren't think what a sharp, broken off branch could do. Sunglasses work on sunny days but aren't so good on duller ones or in dark woods. Go for optics with changeable lenses or even those with Photo Chromatic lenses that react to the available light.

## Pack

Road riders can make do with a banana and a tenner stuffed in a pocket but they are by definition close to a road and other facilities. At 600m on a Lakeland fell, you need to be completely self-sufficient so a pack is essential. Go for a narrow, lightweight cycling or running style pack rather than a walking one. Make sure it will sit nice and stable when the straps are done up, and make sure it has a pocket for a hydration bladder that'll allow you to drink on the move. See below for what to carry.

# WHAT TO CARRY

You've got a pack, what do you need to put in it? Everybody has a different view on this, and it could vary a little between short, low rides e.g. Loughrigg Terrace and mega epics such as Nan Bield. The following is recommended for the bigger or more remote routes, but it also gives an inventory to pick and choose from according to the route/weather/time of year and who you are riding with.

## Spare Clothing

One layer such a fleece or windshirt plus a waterproof (in winter possibly more)

## Puncture Repair

At least one tube each (two on epics), patches, trail pump and tyre levers

## Tools

Cycling multi-tool with chain splitter, spanners, Allen keys, screw driver, spoke key.

Leatherman type multi-tool (one between a group is ok).

Plenty of duct tape—wrap it around your pump, or strips on the inside your pack, or just carry a very small roll.

*A prize for spotting the kitchen sink*

Cable ties… a variety of sizes.

Powerlink for chain—quick way of joining up a chain without a splitter.

Tyre boot for repairing torn tyres.

Shock pump between group.

**Navigation Equipment**
Compass, 1:25,000 map (even if carrying a GPS)

**Mobile Phone**
Carry at least one between two, preferably one each—see notes on **Safety/ Accidents**—and make sure it's fully charged before setting off.

**First Aid Kit**
It's advisable to carry at a small first aid kit—or at least one between two. A small off the shelf kit is ok or build your own using anti-inflammatory drugs/pain killers, antiseptic wipes, gauze pads, sticky plaster (as well as loads of duct tape already mentioned) and a knife or scissors (possibly part of Leatherman or Multi-tool).

*Typical Lake District weather—will it? Or won't it?*

Note: Some first aid training would be a massive help and is recommended for all mountain bikers.

### Food

Trail snacks, energy gels, bananas: whatever your poison really. On an Epic take some sandwiches too.

### Emergencies

Have at least one small light with you always—it's impossible to read a map in the dark. If you think you may be up against it, take a headtorch each and possibly a group shelter. But it's better to just start earlier than go to these extremes.

### Money

A tenner and a credit card weigh little but could be useful in an emergency or just to buy tea and cakes at an unexpected café.

## WEATHER

Always get an up to date weather forecast, preferably one for the mountains, before setting out and take notice of it (weather forecast details are included at the back of the book). If it looks like being a bad day, rethink your plans and stay low. Consider not just the weather but also the temperature and wind strength and direction. Windchill can reduce the ambient temperature by as much as 10°C on an averagely windy day and riding straight into horizontal rain is incredibly sapping and potentially dangerous. In summer, consider the effect of the sun and the temperature and make sure you take sunscreen and plenty of water.

Mountains can be dangerous places, if in any doubt, leave your chosen route for another day.

## SAFETY/ACCIDENT

A mobile phone is always going to be your best bet here, although you may have to go and look for signal—usually on a ridge or summit. For that reason make sure you have one or more phones between you and that they are fully charged before setting out.

If you have an accident, simply dial 999 and ask for Mountain Rescue. Make

*Ouch… take care out there*

*Flats: unavoidable but usually dealt with quickly with the right gear*

sure you can give them an accurate grid reference of where the casualty can be found, also as much detail as possible of the injuries.

An emergency SMS text message service is also available and could be a life saver if your battery is low or you have limited signal, but in order to use it, you must register beforehand. See details in the back of the book for how to register.

Hopefully at least one of you has some first aid skill and will be able to make the casualty as comfortable as possible while you wait.

Remember that for safety purposes, you're definitely better off in numbers: two is better than one; and three or even four is definitely best of all. That way, if something does go wrong, someone can stay with a casualty while the other/s go for help. If you are short of numbers, try and solicit help from others in the area. This is where the whistle can come in handy. Remember six short blasts, with a minute in between means you need help (three short blasts is the usual response but don't stop if you hear this, continue to signal to help others locate you).

# TRAIL FIXES

The usual spoiler of a good ride is a mechanical. Obviously learn as much as you can about maintaining your bike before setting off but the following could get you home if the worst does happen on the trail.

## Punctures

Spare tubes are always the best and quickest way to deal with flats on the trail. Patches make a good backup if you use all your tubes. If you end up out of both tubes and patches, try cutting the tube right through at the puncture then tying a knot in each end. Thread the now linear tube back into the tyre and pump it up carefully before proceeding even more carefully.

## Split Tyre

A tyre boot is best—simply glue it over the split. If you don't have one, anything reasonably flexible but tough will do the job. Try a map cover or cut a piece of plastic from a bottle or something similar. Duct tape will hold it in place while you put the tube back in and put some air in it.

## Broken Chain

The secret here is a powerlink. If you have one, it'll be quite easy although you'll probably need to press the broken link out with your splitter before you can use it. If you don't have one, simply press the rivet two-thirds of the way out and then twist/pull/force the inside link to get it apart. Then press the two ends together so the protruding rivet holds them in the right place, and use the splitter to press the rivet the rest of the way in.

## Broken Freewheel

Use cable ties to join the cassette to the spokes. The resulting fixed-wheel bike should get you home.

## Broken Cables

A broken gear cable will mean either granny ring at the front or top at the rear. To get a better spread, use the high/low adjuster screws to get the chain to the middle.

## Gear Hanger

If it's bent, try and bend it back gently—even bad shifting is better than none. If it's broken, it's time to go singlespeed—at the rear anyway. Probably best to split the chain then take the derailleur out. Now either wrap it around the biggest sprockets front and back and have a real singlespeed, or shorten it and wrap it around the middle, giving you the option of shifting at the front.

## Sticking Brakes

These can usually be adjusted by loosening the caliper Allen screws and realigning the caliper/pads. If you've warped the disc really badly, try straightening it as best you can by trial and error. If you're really struggling with one end, it may be worth prising the pads apart and then not using that brake anymore. It's usually best to remove the lever, or tape it to stop you grabbing it accidentally.

## MAPS

Although we've included 1:50,000 mapping in this book, they are cropped quite tight and won't help if you stray out of them. For that reason, carry a full map or a print out of one that covers a lot of the ground around them. The recommended maps for the area covered in this book are as follows.

### Ordnance Survey

1:25,000 Explorer OL4 The English Lakes North-western area
1:25,000 Explorer OL5 The English Lakes North-eastern area
1:25,000 Explorer OL6 The English Lakes South-western area
1:25,000 Explorer OL7 The English Lakes South-eastern area
1:25,000 Explorer OL19 Howgill Fells and Upper Eden Valley

### Harvey

1:25,000 Superwalker Lakeland North
1:25,000 Superwalker Lakeland Central
1:25,000 Superwalker Lakeland East
1:25,000 Superwalker Lakeland West
1:25,000 Superwalker Lakeland South West
1:25,000 Superwalker Lakeland South East

### British Mountain Maps

1:40,000 Lake District

*Heathery singletrack on the Blawith Fells*

### Grizedale & Windermere

| | | | |
|---|---|---|---|
| 1. | Hawkshead & Grizedale East | 16.5km/10 miles | Medium |
| 2. | Grizedale & Low Parkamoor | 27km/17 miles | Hard |
| 3. | West of Windermere | 13km/8 miles | Easy |

### Staveley & Kentmere Fells

| | | | |
|---|---|---|---|
| 4. | The Garburn Pass | 18km/12 miles | Medium |
| 5. | The Green Quarter | 22km/13 miles | Medium |
| 6. | The Nan Bield Pass | 39km/22 miles | Epic |

# THE SOUTH EAST

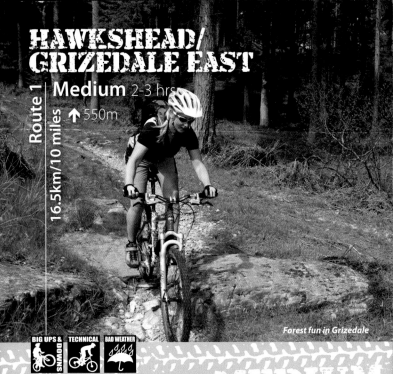

# HAWKSHEAD/ GRIZEDALE EAST

**Route 1**

**16.5km/10 miles**

## Medium 2-3 hrs

↑ 550m

*Forest fun in Grizedale*

**BIG UPS & DOWNS** · **TECHNICAL** · **BAD WEATHER**

## MEDIUM

### IN BRIEF

The natural trails of the **Grizedale Forest** are every bit as good as the manmade ones, and definitely earn their place in this book. This gem kicks off to the east of the forest, making the most of the parking and facilities of **Hawkshead**. It then gets most of the early climbing out of the way in one single tarmac pull up past **Moor Top**. The fire road that follows disappoints momentarily but quickly turns into great singletrack and a real, rough and ready descent down to **Esthwaite Hall**. The next leg follows the same pattern and although the climb's a little easier, the descent's another peach. Road work leads to **Near Sawrey** and the biggest pull of the whole ride, which passes three great tarns before finally relenting high on **Claife Heights**. It gets better and better from here and the final plummet back to **Hawkshead** is just dessert for all that hard work.

MEDIUM

## NEAR SAWREY

This tiny Lakeland hamlet is best known for its connection with Beatrice Potter, who's home, **Hill Top**, is passed on the ride. As well as the wonderful array of beautifully illustrated books that the author became famous for, she also earned a place in the history of the fells being responsible for the survival of the iconic Herdwick Sheep breed that is now synonymous with the area. If you're not sure what you're looking for, they are the generally grey-coloured sheep you'll see on most of the rides in the book.

## THE ROUTE   Start: **Main car cark, Hawkshead** (GR: SD 353 980)

**START**   Turn **L** out of car park and **L** again at top. Continue for 300m and turn **L** *(Grizedale)* to climb steeply. Keep around to the **R** after 300m and then swing **L** to continue climbing all the way to the top. Pass a footpath on the **L**, then **Moor Top** car park on your **R**, and then, turn **L** onto broad track, going around a barrier.

*By Moss Eccles Tarn*

*By Wise Een Tarn*

**2.** Follow the main forest track along, dropping all the time, and after exactly 1km, where the track bends **L**, keep **SA** onto a singletrack bridleway. Follow this to the end and bear **L** onto a stony track that drops down through the woods to a road at the bottom. Turn **R** and climb steeply up, eventually cresting the rise and dropping again. After 1.7km of road, look for a waymarked BW on the **L** (sharp **L** easy to miss).

**3.** Follow the grassy track across a field to a gate. Go through and climb up through the forest, keeping **SA** at a x-roads of trails. This leads to another great descent and eventually the road. Turn **R** and then next **L** to climb up to **Near Sawrey**. Keep **R** on entering the village and

**R** again on the main road. And then, after 100m, turn **L** onto a narrow lane.

4. Follow this up through gates, merging with a track from the **R** and then keeping **R** to climb to **Moss Eccles Tarn**. Keep ahead

with the lake to your **L** and keep **L** at a fork to continue to a gate above **Wise Een Tarn**. Keep **SA** to a gate on the edge of the forest. Keep **SA** for 200m and bear **L** onto an easy-to-miss BW.

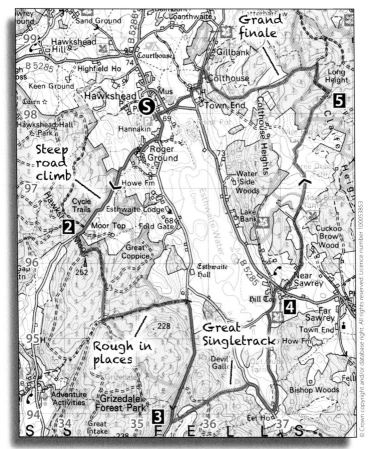

*Rocky horror show near Devil's Gallop*

**5.** Follow this down, straight-across another track and then down again to a junction where you bear sharp **L** to climb steeply up and around to the **R**. Continue **SA** at a x-roads and continue over the top and down out of the forest, enjoying a long descent all the way down to the road. Turn **L** and then **R** and **R** again back to **Hawkshead**. Cross the bridge and turn **R** to the car park.

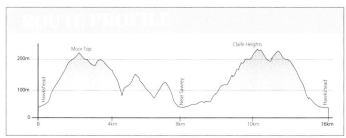

ROUTE PROFILE

**NEED TO KNOW**

**Start/Finish:** Main car park, Hawkshead
**Grid ref:** SD 353 980; **Approx postcode:** LA22 0NT
**Nearest town:** Windermere
**Total distance:** 16.5km/10 miles
**Total ascent:** 550m
**Approx time:** 2-3hrs
**OS Map:** OL6 *The English Lakes South-eastern Area*
**Refreshments:** *Tower Bank Arms* at *Near Sawrey* is just off the route; loads of choice in *Hawkshead*.
**Best time:** Generally good surfaces and not too exposed to bad weather. Popular with walkers in places.
**Want more:** Easy link with **Route 3** or a more complex one with **Route 2**: simply bear right instead of left at the junction of singletrack and stony track after **point 2**. This leads to the main **Visitor Centre**, which is also the start of **The North Face trails**.
**Weekend away:** Obvious bundles with **Routes 3** and **2** and The North Face trail, but base yourself a little further north and you're in the middle of the **Loughrigg** and **Hodge Close** loops (**7, 8** & **9**) and good for the **Coniston** routes (**11, 12** & **13**).

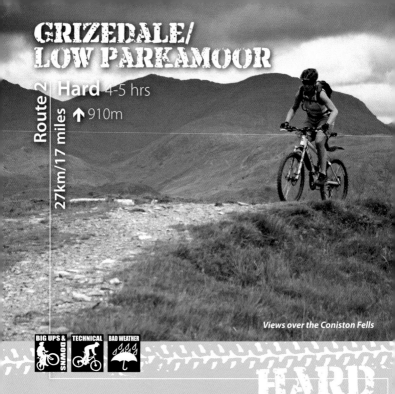

# GRIZEDALE/ LOW PARKAMOOR

**Route 2**

**Hard** 4-5 hrs

↑910m

27km/17 miles

*Views over the Coniston Fells*

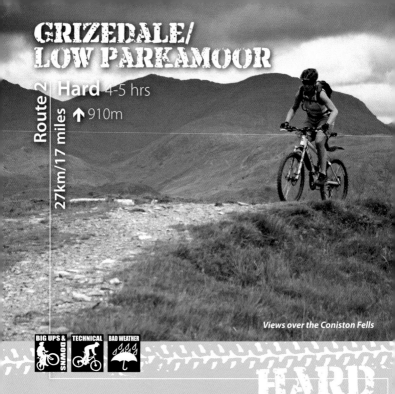

BIG UPS & DOWNS | TECHNICAL | BAD WEATHER

HARD

## IN BRIEF

This route links some of the excellent 'natural' trails in the forest with some full-on rock-strewn tracks to the south, making a short, sharp and challenging loop that'll 'go' in pretty much any weather or conditions. It starts with a steep yet rideable pull up from **Waterhead** into the forest and then follows easy tracks out to the remote farmstead of **Low Parkamoor**, where the fun really starts. The descent combines some of the best riding in the area with some amazing views over **Coniston Water** to the Coniston Fells. The wonderfully-named **Bletherbarrow Lane** leads from **Nibthwaite** back into the trees and top-notch rollercoaster trails then loop north, above the **Visitor Centre**, before clambering back up on to **Grizedale Moor** for a fitting grand finale. The drop past **Lawson Park** is a beauty: an exquisite cocktail of roots, rocks, twists and turns that eventually deliver you back to the lake shore.

# CONISTON WATER

At 8km long and 800m wide, **Coniston Water** is Lakeland's third largest lake and is also one of the most handsome, especially from the south or east, where it's framed by the impressive Coniston Fells. It's a magnet for outdoor sports of all sorts these days, but it's probably best known for its association with Malcolm and Donald Campbell's attempts on the World Water Speed Record. Sadly Donald was killed in 1967 after recording a run of over 320mph

# THE ROUTE   Start: **Waterhead** car park; (GR: SD 316 978)

**START.** Turn **R** out of the car park and climb up to a T-junction, where you turn **R**. Continue for 200m to a waymarked BW on the **L** (opposite a house). Climb the main track, ignoring two **L** forks and keeping **SA** through a gate that leads back into the forest. Continue up to a T-junction with a forest track and turn **R**.

**2.** Climb to a junction with a BW *(Moor Top)*, which you ignore, and continue a few metres to a

*Rock 'n' roll on the descent to Nibthwaite*

major junction, where you fork **R**. Now follow this for around 1.4km to a sharp **LH** bend, where you keep **SA**. Follow this out of the forest and **SA** to drop to **Low Parkamoor**.

**3.** Climb away from the building and bear **R** onto a broad track. Follow this for over 3km to the road where you turn **L**. Continue for 1.8km and bear **L** into a narrow lane by farm buildings.

**4.** Climb steeply to a gate and way-marked junction. Fork **R** towards Ickenthwaite and then drop to the road, where you turn **L**. Drop to a T-junction and bear **L** again. Now continue for 600m to a BW on the **L**.

**5.** Climb to the top and bear **L**. Continue for 1km to a car park on the **L** and turn **L** onto a stony BW. Follow this to the edge of the forest and keep **R** to climb up to a broad forest track.

*Singletrack near Low Parkamoor*

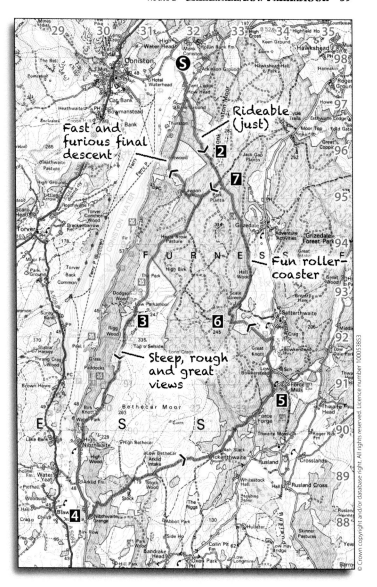

Rideable (just)

Fast and furious final descent

Fun roller-coaster

Steep, rough and great views

*Spring in Grizedale*

**6.** Bear **R** onto this, drop to cross a stream and climb past two turnings on the **L**. Continue for 2km, passing turnings on the **R** to **Grizedale Forest Centre**. Then turn **L**, above the centre, onto a waymarked stony bridleway climb. Climb to a junction with a track and bear **R** to the junction you visited earlier.

**7.** Turn **L** for 400m and bear **R** onto a waymarked BW. Drop to the clearing and keep **SA** to

contour around **Crag Head** and down to the road. Turn **R,** then **L** to return to the car park.

## NEED TO KNOW

**Start/Finish:** Waterhead car park
**Grid ref:** SD 316 978; **Approx postcode:** LA21 8AA
**Nearest town:** Coniston
**Total distance:** 27km/17 miles
**Total ascent:** 910m
**Approx time:** 4-5hrs
**OS Map:** OL6 *The English Lakes South-eastern Area*

**Refreshments:** None on route; but you could drop to the **Forest Centre** in Grizedale.

**Best time:** Generally good surfaces and not too exposed to bad weather, although the section down from Parkamoor is quite exposed. Popular with walkers in places.

**Want more:** The obvious extension here is to link this one with **Round Coniston (Route 13)** to make a tough day out. It could also be linked with **Route 1** or even **The North Face trail**—best option here is to join it at point 7 and complete the man-made trail before the final descent of this one .

**Weekend away:** Base yourself around Coniston and you're spot on for the two Coniston starts (**Routes 11 & 13**) and not far off **Route 12** as well. The **Hawkshead** and **Loughrigg loops** aren't out of the question either.

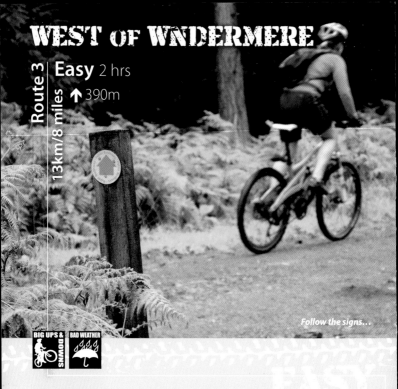

# WEST OF WNDERMERE

**BIG UPS & DOWNS**

**BAD WEATHER**

*Follow the signs...*

EASY

## IN BRIEF

Not all Lakes' mountain biking is epic. And not all loops climb high. So when the weather suggests a big outing over the fells is out of the question, it's always good to have something short and sharp to fall back on—even if it's just to justify an afternoon spent in the pub. This is a sweet little number really. Tagging it as Easy doesn't really do justice to the excellent riding on offer; technical and all-consuming, even if it is quite short. It starts steep—thankfully on asphalt—but after that initial climb it's more about balance and line choice than legs and lungs and only the best will clean it all. The highlights are the descents—no surprise there then—the first past a succession of tarns on the only stretch without tree cover; and the second, a wickedly wonderful plummet to the shores of the lake at the end.

EASY

# WINDERMERE

**Windermere** or Lake Windermere? It's the subject of much debate. Either way at 17km long, over 1.5km wide and over 70m deep, it is undoubtedly the largest natural lake in England. It is also the name of the town on the eastern shores, which in turn is connected to **Bowness-on-Windermere**, a true Lakeland tourist trap.

# THE ROUTE   Start: **Red Nab** car park (GR: SD 385 994)

**START**   Turn **R** out of the car park and climb steeply on tarmac to a T-junction at the top. Turn **L** for a few metres and then turn **L** again onto a broad drive *(Basecamp)*. Follow this up and then fork **R**, through a gate, onto a waymarked BW.

**2.** Follow this into the woods, eventually bearing **R** off the main track and crossing open ground to join another broad track. Bear sharp **R** onto this and follow it for around 500m to a sharp **L**. Take this and continue to a x-roads at Guide Posts.

*Above Wise Een Tarn*

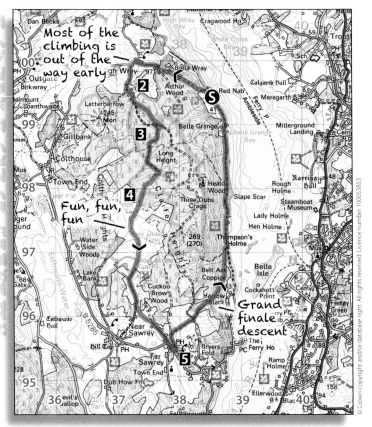

Most of the climbing is out of the way early

Fun, fun, fun

Grand finale descent

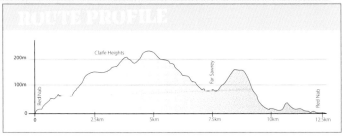

**ROUTE PROFILE**

**3.** Keep **SA** here and continue **SA** at another forest track to another x-roads, where you turn **R** *(The Sawreys)* to follow a rough track to a better track, which you turn **R** onto to follow it to a gate that leads onto open ground.

**4.** Now follow the obvious main track down past **Wise Een Tarn** and **Moss Eccles Tarn**, and then, 500m after the latter, bear **L** at a fork *(Far Sawrey)* to drop to the road at **Far Sawrey**. Turn **L** and drop to the Sawrey Hotel, where you turn **L** onto a **BW**.

**5.** Now climb up through a gate before forking **R**. Continue up through two gates and then start to drop back into woodland. Descend all the way to the shores of **Windermere**, where you turn **L** to follow the clear trail back to the car park.

## NEED TO KNOW

**Start/Finish:** Red Nab car park
**Grid ref:** SD 385 994; **Approx postcode:** LA22 0JH
**Nearest town:** Windermere
**Total distance:** 13km/8 miles
**Total ascent:** 390m
**Approx time:** 2hrs
**OS Map:** OL6 *The English Lakes South-eastern Area*
**Refreshments:** Sawrey Hotel, on the route.
**Best time:** Staying low and mainly in the trees this makes a good all-weather ride. The trails will be slippery and a little more technical in the wet. Popular with walkers.
**Want more:** This loop connects quite easily to the **Hawkshead** and **Grizedale East** outing (**Route 1**) and that in turn can be linked to the **Grizedale and Low Parkamoor route** (**Route 2**). Or pushing things further, that can be taken around Coniston Water by linking it with the **Round Coniston** route (**Route 13**). How far can you go?
**Weekend away:** The obvious bundles are the two **Grizedale loops** (**Routes 1** & **2**) but base yourself between here and Ambleside and the **Loughrigg and Hodge Close routes** (**7, 8** & **9**) would make good partners too. Or there's **The North Face trail**.

# THE GARBURN PASS

**BEST DESCENT**

**TOP FIVE**

*Great riding and chocolate box scenery*

BIG UPS & DOWNS · TECHNICAL · MOUNTAIN

**MEDIUM**

## IN BRIEF

A real fast food version of one of the great Lakes' passes, but still no pushover and only the best will clean it all. The early stages are easy-angled and a good warm up. And there's nothing too testing until you're almost there. But a short, sharp and extremely loose and rocky ramp will probably put pay to most attempts, and then it's all about damage limitation. And skill and bravery on the descent. It's not too bad really: more bark than bite. But it still needs commitment—give the horse its head—and line choice is everything on the crux sections, which really are steep. The bottom third is more uncomfortable than challenging but don't drop your guard too early: it would be a crime to blow it now. The homeward leg is just plain fun, and would be memorable on its own on any other day.

**MEDIUM**

# THE GARBURN PASS

The pass itself is a lofty saddle that splits the rocky tops at the southern end of the **Kentmere Horseshoe**. The road that hurdles the pass was once a main thoroughfare between **Troutbeck** and **Kentmere**, from where it led on towards **Shap** and the north.

# THE ROUTE   Start: **Ings** (GR: SD 443 987)

**START**   Cross the road and bear immediately **R** onto a narrow lane: *Moor Howe Road*. Follow this easily up passing a turning on the **L** at **Mislet** and two further turnings on the **L** before turning **R** onto a broad track *(Dubbs Road)*. Keep **SA** past **Dubbs Reservoir**, until you reach a junction with the **Garburn Pass** track.

**2.** Bear **R** onto it and climb steeply to the pass, where you go through a gate and descend steeply until you eventually reach farm buildings at the **Nook**. Bear **L** to the road and then follow this down into Kentmere and past the church to a junction with a tarmac drive on the **R**.

**3.** Take this (sharp **R**) and then follow it past a footpath on the **L** and **Kentmere Hall** on the **R**. Keep **L**, through a gate, and climb steeply on a good track.

*An easier section on the climb up to the Garburn Pass*

Follow this for 1.5km around **Whiteside End** and keep **L** at a fork. Continue to a gate and a large stream.

**4.** Cross the stream and keep **SA**, on a good track, which you follow for 2km to a gate and a junction. Bear **L** to **Grassgarth**

and after 500m bear **L** again at another junction to pass beneath **Williamson's Monument**

5. Carry on **SA** to the road at The **Heights** and keep ahead for

200m, where you turn **R** (**SA**) onto a track on a sharp **LH** bend. Stay with this up past a farm, down to a T-junction and turn **R** to the road. Turn **L** to return to the A591 at **Ings**.

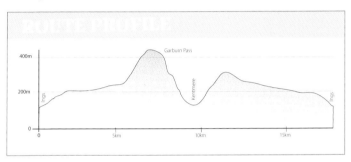

ROUTE PROFILE

Garburn Pass

400m

200m

Ings

Kentmere

Ings

0

0            5km            10km            15km

**NEED TO KNOW**

**Start/Finish:** Ings
**Grid ref:** SD 443 987; **Approx postcode:** LA8 9PS
**Nearest town:** Windermere
**Total distance:** 18km/12 miles
**Total ascent:** 570m
**Approx time:** 2-3hrs
**OS Map:** OL6 *The English Lakes South-eastern Area*
**Refreshments:** None on route; **Watermil Inn**, Ings, **Wilf's Café** at Staveley.
**Best ime:** Mostly good surfaces but some surface water on the final few trails. It climbs quite high so could be grim at the pass in poor weather
**Want more:** The **Nan Bield Pass loop (Route 6)** provides a lengthier alternative. Or if you want to mix and match somewhere in between, perhaps link it with the **Green Quarter (Route 5)** at Kentmere and enjoy a 25km Medium.
**Weekend away:** The **Nan Bield Pass (Route 6)** and the **Green Quarter** loop **(Route 5)** both start around here. Or base yourself nearer to Ambleside where there's loads of choice. You're not far from the **Trail Centre** at **Grizedale** too.

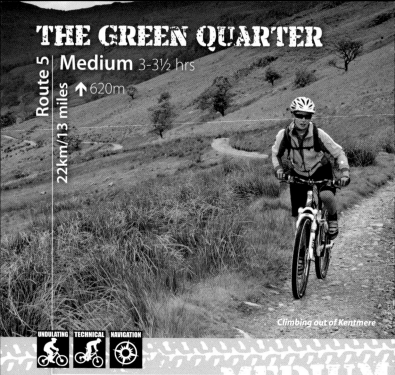

# THE GREEN QUARTER

**Medium** 3-3½ hrs

↑620m

Route 5

22km/13 miles

*Climbing out of Kentmere*

UNDULATING  TECHNICAL  NAVIGATION

MEDIUM

## IN BRIEF

There's a bit of everything in this one; from easy road climbing amid great scenery, to full-on, rock n' roll downhill and a few great sections of sinuous singletrack across some seldom-explored moors. The outward leg is similar to the **Nan Bield loop** (**Route 6**) but no need to hold back on this one: it's a fair bit shorter. And the return leg follows some great moorland singletrack over **Green Quarter**—beware: it will frustrate and exhaust when anything other than bone dry. Highlights include a fast and furious descent to **Kentmere**—the reverse of **Route 4**—and a steeper and even rougher drop into **Longsleddale**—Lakeland mountain biking at its finest. The Green Quarter singletrack gets you singing for your supper and rewards with a few super sweet sections; and the plummet down through the HP plantation to the road rounds the proceedings off nicely.

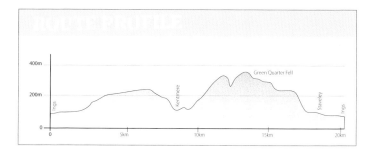

## THE ROUTE  Start: **Ings** (GR: SD 443 987)

**START** Cross the road and head up the lane opposite. Continue to its end and keep **SA** onto a walled BW track that climbs easily up. Keep **L** when another BW joins from the **R** and then bear **R** at a fork after another 500m. Now keep **SA** to follow a well-surfaced track that eventually leads to a ford.

**2.** Cross the river and go through the gate ahead to follow the obvious track alongside a wall. This bears **R** and then **L** to eventually drop steeply down to **Kentmere Hall**. Bear **R** in front of the house and climb up to the road. Turn **R** to drop to **Low Bridge**.

**3.** Turn **L** onto a narrow lane and climb steeply up to a T-junction where you turn **L** to continue climbing to a broad track on the **R** *(Sadgill and Longsleddale)*. Follow this up and then down, until you see a BW marked to the **R**, immediately before a gate (easy to miss).

**4.** Take this, drop to cross a stream and then keep **SA** with the wall to your **L**. Go through another gate and head diagonally up to another gate. Continue in the same direction as the gradient eases and keep **SA** through another gate now to drop past a ruined building to another gate.

**5.** Keep ahead across a corner and keep **L** at a fork by another ruin. Now continue to another gate in a field corner and head

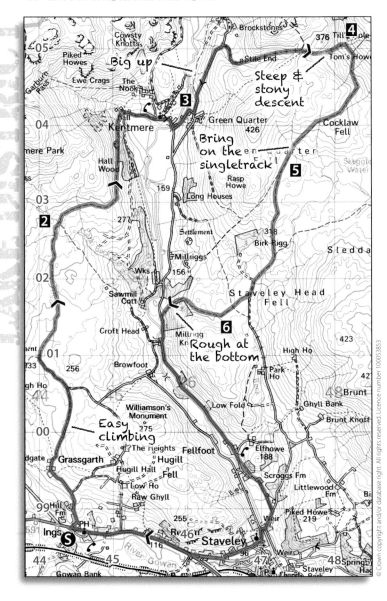

diagonally across this to meet a good track by another gate. Go through this and follow the main track across to a gate on the **R**. Go through and follow the wall along before bearing around to the right after 500m.

**6.** Follow the vague track which improves to a gate and go through to drop sweetly down to the edge of the wood. Keep it your **L** and then bear sharp

**L** to enter the wood and drop steeply down to the road.

**7.** Turn **L** and follow it down for 2km. Just after a turning on the **L**, bear **L** onto a BW that leads to **Scroggs Farm**. Keep **SA** through the farm and turn **R** onto the road. Turn **R** over the bridge and then turn **L** straight after it. Take the first **R** into **Brow Lane** and then turn **R** again, at the end, to finish.

## NEED TO KNOW

**Start/Finish:** Ings
**Grid ref:** SD 443 987; **Approx postcode:** LA8 9QQ
**Nearest town:** Windermere
**Total distance:** 22km/13 miles
**Total ascent:** 620m
**Approx time:** 3-3½hrs
**OS Map:** OL6 *The English Lakes South-eastern Area*
**Refreshments:** None on route; **Watermill Inn**, Ings at finish; **Wilf's Café** at Staveley.
**Best time:** A definite dry weather, summer route—the moorland singletrack that offers such great riding when dry is seriously hard work when wet.
**Want more:** The obvious extension is to have a go at the **Nan Bield Pass** (**Route 6**). But a mix and match with the **Garburn Pass** (**Route 4**) is another option; or head west towards Ambleside on good trails from Troutbeck.
**Weekend away:** Bundle with either the **Nan Bield Pass** (**Route 6**) or **Garburn Pass** (**Route 4**) or base yourself nearer to **Ambleside** where there's loads of choice. You're not far from the **Trail Centre** at **Grizedale** too.

# THE NAN BIELD PASS

**Epic** 6-8 hrs

↑ 1400m

TOP FIVE

*Rough and rocky singletrack*

**BIG UPS & DOWNS** · **TECHNICAL** · **MOUNTAIN** · **NAVIGATION** · **PUSH OR CARRY**

EPIC

## IN BRIEF

This is the toughest of the high pass routes in the book. And one of the toughest loops full stop. But it's a tremendously rewarding ride that penetrates deep into some wild and wonderful scenery. The outward leg is the reverse of the **Garburn Pass** route and just as enjoyable this way round. But this time it's just a warm up and the true meat of the outing is a whole lot more serious. It starts with a rocky horror show drop to **Sadgill**, and a tough but do-able clamber up to **Gatesgarth**. And then the ante is upped even further on the other side: rough and tumble Lakes' mtbing at its very finest. The carry up to the **Nan Bield Pass** is an absolute killer. But it's worth it. The switchback singletrack that greets you is among the best you'll ever ride, and it goes on forever. There are off-road options back to **Staveley** from **Kentmere**, but most will stick to the road.

# NAN BIELD PASS

At well over 600m above sea level, the **Nan Bield Pass** crosses the bounds from a mountain bike trail to a high mountain path and it needs to be treated with respect, especially as it comes so late—there really is no easy escape from **Mardale**. As a gauge, if you find the drop to **Sadgill** beyond you, you're probably best not going any further. Check the weather before setting out, and leave plenty of time. It's also advisable to carry plenty of food and warm clothing.

# THE ROUTE Start: **Staveley** (GR: SD 460 984)

**START** Continue along the deadend road to follow the cycleway along the side of the **A591**. Ignore one turning on the **R** and then take the second (opposite the Ings Village turn). Head up the lane for **400m** then turn **R** onto a broad track. Keep **L** at a fork and **L** again at **The Heights**.

**2.** Keep **SA** past buildings and follow a good track, keeping **SA** at a junction with a road and then keeping **R** at two forks to follow a well-surfaced BW to **Park Beck**. Cross the river and **SA** through a gate to follow the obvious track alongside a wall. This bears **R** and then **L** to drop steeply to **Kentmere Hall**.

**3.** Bear **R** in front of the house and climb up to the road. Turn **R** to drop to **Low Bridge**. Turn **L** onto a narrow lane and climb steeply up to a T-junction

*Cruising near Sadgill*

where you turn **L** to continue climbing to a broad track on the **R** *(Public Byway Sadgill and Longsleddale)*.

**4.** Follow this up and then down, keeping to the main track at a BW junction, to drop to farm buildings at **Sadgill**. Keep **SA** over the bridge and turn **L** onto the broad track beyond. Now follow the track as it climbs steeply up to **Gatesgarth Pass**.

**5.** Keep **SA** to drop steeply towards **Mardale Head** and just before you reach the road head, bear **L** onto a waymarked BW *(Nan Bield)*. Now follow this around the hillside and steeply up to **Small Water**. Keep the lake to your **L** and climb the impossibly steep path to **Nan Bield Pass**.

**6.** Keep **SA** to follow singletrack all the way down into a field

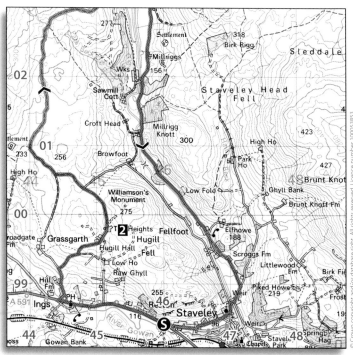

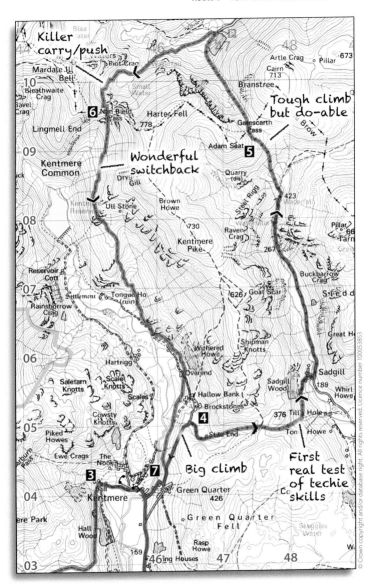

Killer
carry/push

Mardale Ill
Bell
**10**
Bleathwaite
Crag
Gavel
Crag

Blea
Water

Piot Crag

Small
Water

Harter Fell
778

Artle Crag

Pillar
673

Cairn
713

Branstree

Tough climb
but do-able

**6** Nan Bield
Pass

Gatescarth
Pass

Brow

Lingmell End

**09**

Kentmere
Common

Wonderful
switchback

Adam Seat

**5**

ick

Dry
Gill

Quarry
(dis)

**423**

Steel Rigg

**08**

Ull Stone

Brown
Howe

730

Kentmere
Pike

Raven
Crag

267

Waterfall

Pillar

66
Tarn

Grey

**07**

Reservoir
Cott

Settlement

Tongue Ho
(ruin)

626

Goat Scar

Buckbarrow
Crag

S  e  d  d

Rainsborrow
Crag

**06**

Hartrigg

Scalet
Knotts

Withered
Howe

Shipman
Knotts

Great H

Saletarn
Knotts

Scales

Overend

Sadgill
Wood

Sadgill
189

Whirl
Howe

**05**

Cowsty
Knotts

Hallow Bank

Brockstones

**4**

376

Till's Hole

Ton

Howe

Piked
Howes

Ewe Crags

The
Nook

**7**

Stile End

Big climb

First
real test
of techie
skills

**3**

ere Park

Kentmere

Green Quarter
426

G  r  e  e  n    Q  u  a  r  t  e  r
Fell

Skeggles
Water

Hall
Wood

159

**46**

Rasp
Howe

ng Houses

**47**

**48**

W.

system. Keep high when you see a good track down below and you'll soon drop to farm buildings at **Overend**. Turn **R** though a gate onto a **BW** beyond the farm and follow this down and then briefly up to join the road.

**7.** Turn **R** to retrace your earlier tracks to Low Bridge and then turn **L** to follow the road all the way down the dale to Staveley. Bear **L** after crossing the bridge and then take the first **R** *(Brow Lane)*. This T's into another road where you turn **R** to the finish.

## ROUTE PROFILE

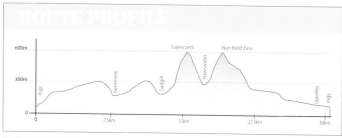

## NEED TO KNOW

**Start/Finish:** Staveley
**Grid ref:** SD 460 984; **Approx postcode:** LA8 9PS
**Nearest town:** Windermere
**Total distance:** 39km/22 miles
**Total ascent:** 1400m
**Approx time:** 6-8hrs
**OS Map:** OL6 *The English Lakes South-eastern Area*
**Refreshments:** None on route; **Eagle & Child**, Staveley, **Wilf's Café** at Staveley, **Watermill Inn**, Ings.
**Best time:** Good surfaces but not a ride to be done in bad weather. Check the weather carefully and start early in winter—people get rescued from this ride.
**Want more:** Link the northern loop with the **Garburn Pass (Route 4)** to make a seriously challenging 'Three Lakeland Passes' route.
**Weekend away:** The **Garburn Pass (Route 4)** and **Green Quarter (Route 5)** routes start nearby but cover a lot of the same ground. An **Ambleside** base would open up a host of possibilities. You're not far from the **Trail Centre** at **Grizedale** too.

*Great riding and views of the Langdale Pikes*

## Ambleside & The Langdales

## Coniston Area

## Western Esoteria

# THE SOUTH WEST

# LOUGHRIGG FELL/ THE LANGDALES

**Route 7**

**25km/16 miles** ↑940m

**Hard** 4 hrs

## TOP FIVE

*Typical Lakes' scenery*

BIG UPS & DOWNS · TECHNICAL · BAD WEATHER

HARD

## IN BRIEF

This is without a doubt the best of the lower-level loops in this book. And it goes in pretty much any weather too—perfect for winter. There's quite a bit of climbing involved, and it's a pretty techie outing too, with some wonderful rocky sections to negotiate—both up and down. The opening run across **Loughrigg Fell** sets the tone well: a steep up followed by a rough and ready crossing of some sublimely gorgeous scenery. After that it's up to **Arnside** and a rock and roll rollercoaster to **Hodge Close**. A slaty descent follows—atmospheric beyond belief. It's big up and a big down from **High Tilberthwaite**: the up's nigh on impossible—elite athletes only—but the descent's a dream if you like it rocky. The drop to **Elterwater** shouldn't present too many problems but the pull up again might just be a hill too far for tired legs. Hopefully not: there's more good stuff to follow…

HARD

# THE ROUTE  Start: **Rydal Water** car park (GR: SD 364 059)

**START**  Turn **R** onto the road and follow it for nearly 2km to a waymarked BW on the **R** (cattle grid). Now climb steeply past **Brow Head Farm** and out on to **Loughrigg Fell**. Continue **SA** to the top and then stay on the main track eventually following a wall on your **L**.

2. Keep **SA** where another BW forks **L** through a gate and continue to a x-roads with a broad track. Keep **SA** along another broad track and swing **L** to the road. Turn **R** and then **L** to drop steeply to the **A593**.

3. Turn **R** towards **Coniston** and continue steeply up for 1.3km to a gate on the **L** that leads onto a very rough track *(bridleway)*. Now climb steeply on rock and grass to a gap in a wall. Turn **L** after this and continue up to a gate.

4. Now descend to another gate and a T-junction, where you

*Near Iron Keld*

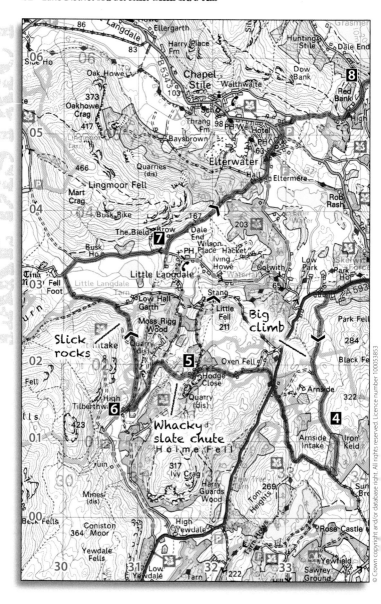

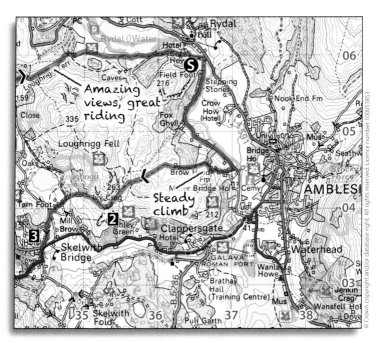

turn **R**. Follow this all the way down to the road again and go **SA** across to climb then drop to **High Oxen Farm**. Keep **SA** through a gate and climb then drop to a T-junction at the hamlet of **Hodge Close**.

**5.** Turn **L** then **R** then **L** again through the houses and then turn **R** through a gate and drop to a sunken BW that descends through the slate to a bridge. Continue up to a junction and turn **L** for 1km to a gate that

leads into the farm buildings at **High Tilberthwaite**.

**6.** Turn sharp **R** through another gate and climb steeply on a rough track. Keep ahead as it descends and ignore a **R** turning to drop onto a rough track all the way to the road. Turn **R** and then **R** again and then follow the road for 1.4km to a turning on the **L** *(Challenging Cycle Path to Ambleside)*.

*High on Loughrigg Fell*

**7.** Climb and then drop, ignoring a BW to the **L**, all the way to road near **Elterwater**. Turn **L** to the village and keep **L** at the fork by the Britannia Inn to the B5343. Keep **SA** across the road and now climb steeply, keeping **R** at the first junction and **L** at the top. Continue to a BW on the **R** (*Loughrigg Terrace and Rydal*).

**8.** Follow this down, passing above **Grasmere** and then dropping to the shores of **Rydal Water**—care is needed on this section as it is narrow and often very busy. Keep ahead, over the rocks, and then stay on the main track as it climbs slightly to a gate before dropping to the car park.

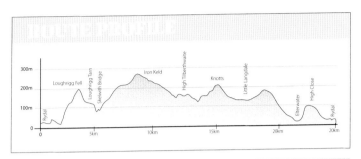

**NEED TO KNOW**

**Start/Finish:** Rydal Water car park
**Grid ref:** NY 364 059; **Approx postcode:** LA22 9LW
**Nearest town:** Ambleside
**Total distance:** 25km/16 miles
**Total ascent:** 940m
**Approx time:** 4hrs
**OS Map:** OL6 *The English Lakes South-eastern Area*

**Refreshments:** The Britannia Inn at **Elterwater** is on the route late on, or the
**Three Shires Inn** at **Little Langdale** is close by at **Point 7**.

**Best time:** Well-drained, firm trails that will work all year round and not too
exposed to the weather either. A great winter outing.

**Want more:** It is possible to slip south towards **Hawkshead** and **Route 1** from
High Arnside (after **Point 4**), but it's a tough outing already.

**Weekend away:** An **Ambleside** base works for this plus its little brother (**Route
8**), and won't be bad for **Grizedale** and **Routes 1 & 2** too.

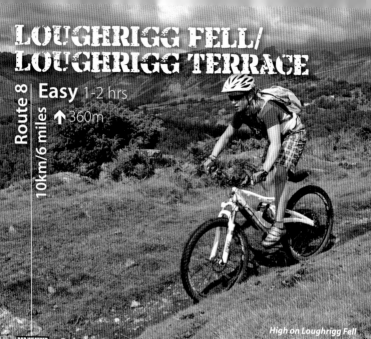

# LOUGHRIGG FELL/ LOUGHRIGG TERRACE

**Easy** 1-2 hrs

↑360m

*High on Loughrigg Fell*

BAD WEATHER

EASY

## IN BRIEF

This route could definitely be called '**Loughrigg Lite**' in comparison to **Route 7**, but this wouldn't really do justice to a superb little loop in just 10km takes in a little of everything that's good about Lakeland mountain biking. It may be short but it's definitely no pushover. It's basically a two-up, two-down; with the first and toughest climb coming early onto **Loughrigg Fell**, and the second, which is much easier, on tarmac at the halfway point. Both the descents are full-on fun but the roller-coaster ride along **Loughrigg Terrace** is one of the best in the book: sweet easy rolling in some places and a real rocky horror shows in others. A word of warning: the terrace gets extremely busy with walkers so choose your day carefully or better still avoid busy periods altogether. And always ride with something in reserve.

EASY

# GRASMERE

Described by poet, William Wordsworth, as *"the loveliest spot that man hath ever found,"* **Grasmere** is indeed one of the Lake District's most scenic lakes. Wordsworth actually lived in **Dove Cottage**, in the village, which is open to the public and is definitely worth a visit if time allows. Neighbouring **Rydal Water** is equally as stunning.

## THE ROUTE   Start: **Rydal Water** car park (GR: NY 364 059)

**START**  Turn **R** onto the road and follow it for nearly 2km to a waymarked, tarmac BW on the **R** (cattle grid). Now climb steeply up past **Brow Head Farm** and out on to **Loughrigg Fell**. Continue **SA** to the top and then stay on the main track eventually following a wall on your **L**.

**2.** Keep **SA** where another BW forks **L** through a gate and continue to a x-roads with a broad track. Keep **SA** along another broad track and swing

*Wonderful views and riding on Loughrigg Terrace*

*It's easy to see why Wordsworth loved this view so much*

**L** to the road. Turn **R** and cruise up past Loughrigg Tarn and then fork **R**. Continue to the top, pass a small road on the **L**, and a footpath on the **R**, and then fork **R** onto a BW (*Loughrigg Terrace and Rydal*).

**3.** Follow this down, passing above **Grasmere** and then dropping to the shores of **Rydal Water**—care is needed on this section as it is narrow and often very busy. Keep ahead, over the rocks, and then stay on the main track as it climbs slightly to a gate before dropping to the car park.

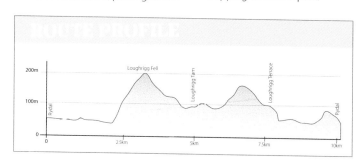

ROUTE PROFILE

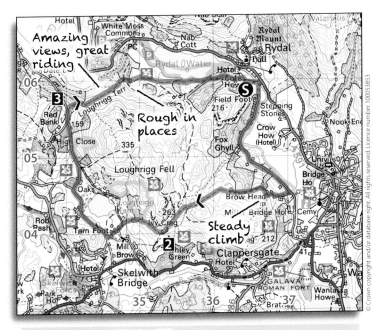

## NEED TO KNOW

**Start/Finish:** Rydal Water car park

**Grid ref:** NY 364 059; **Approx postcode:** LA22 9LW

**Nearest town:** Ambleside

**Total distance:** 10km/6 miles

**Total ascent:** 360m

**Approx time:** 1-2hrs

**OS Map:** OL6 *The English Lakes South-eastern Area*

**Refreshments:** Come on! nobody needs refreshments on a ride this short? Head into **Rydal** or **Ambleside** if you're desperate.

**Best time:** Well-drained, firm trails that will work all year round.

**Want more:** Route 7 is basically a longer version, just follow that.

**Weekend away:** An **Ambleside** base works for this or its big brother (**Route 7**), and won't be bad for **Grizedale** and Routes 1 & 2 as well.

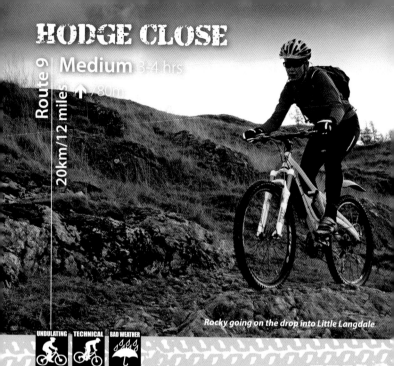

# HODGE CLOSE

## Medium 3-4 hrs

*Rocky going on the drop into Little Langdale*

UNDULATING  TECHNICAL  BAD WEATHER

MEDIUM

## IN BRIEF

This route could be looked on as a shorter, easier version of the **Loughrigg & the Langdales** loop (**Route 7**), but it doesn't actually go as far north as even Little Langdale let alone Loughrigg, and it also tackles many of the trails in the reverse direction making it a very different ride and well worth doing whether you've ticked the longer route or not. It could probably win the award for the most contrived route in the book, with three distinctly different loops linked in such a way that each trail is ridden in the best direction. It doesn't look pretty on the map but it certainly shows the amount of effort that goes into getting the best out of a route. Highlights include the fast and furious drop into **Little Langdale** and the twists and turns from **High Arnside**; but pretty much every metre is good fun and every trail earns its place.

MEDIUM

# HODGE CLOSE

**Hodge Close Quarry** is one of many slate workings in the **Tilberthwaite Valley** and was actually operating right up until the 1960s. The quarry itself is a huge excavation which drops almost 100m from ground level. The steep walls are home to a number of rock climbs and the flooded workings are extremely popular with cave divers.

# THE ROUTE (Start: **Tilberthwaite** car park (GR: NY 306 009)

**START** Turn **L** out of the car park and continue to the farmyard, where you keep **SA** through the gate on the **L**. Climb then descend to a junction (easy to miss), where you turn sharp **R**. Follow this to a bridge and ford on your **L** and turn **R**. Fork immediately **R** *(Coniston via Tilberthwaite)*.

**2.** Follow this to the first track on the **L** (no waymark at time of writing) and drop to cross a slate bridge then climb through spoil to a T-junction at the top. Turn **L** and then turn **R** between the houses. At the end, swing **L** again onto a track and then turn almost immediately **R** to climb to gate.

*Rollercoaster riding from Iron Keld*

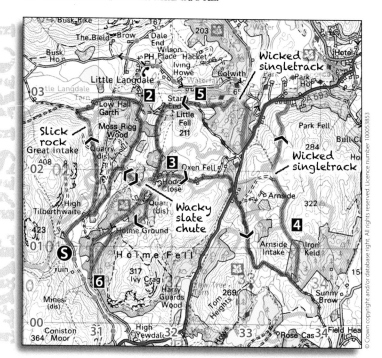

**3.** Keep **SA** now to High Oxen Farm and bear **R** onto a lane. Follow this to the A593 and ride **SA** onto a steep drive (*High Arnside*). Ride up the drive and keep R where it bears **L** (*Knipe Fold*). Now keep **SA** for 1.5km to a BW on the **L** (*Iron Keld*). Climb on a good track and then at the top keep **L** (*BW Iron Keld*).

**4.** Now follow the BW down, staying on the main track the whole time. Continue to the

A593 and turn **L** to ride up past the **Eskdale** turn and past a wood on the **R**. Take the first turning on the **R**. Turn straightaway **R** through a gate onto a **National Trust Cycle Trail** and drop down to a junction by a gate. Turn **L** onto a BW and follow this up to a gate that leads out of woods and on to **High Park Farm**.

**5.** Turn **L** to the top of drive and then **R** to **Stang End Farm**. Turn

L here onto a steep concrete ramp and continue up to a gate. Go through and then turn **L** to the gate you passed through earlier. Go through and turn **R** this time *(Holme Ground, Yewdale)* and then follow this up and then down to the road.

**6.** Turn **R** and ride up to the junction at **Hodge Close**, where you turn **L** to retrace your earlier tracks back down the slate track to the junction above the bridge. Turn **L** here to **High Tilberthwaite Farm** and keep **SA** to continue down the road to the car park.

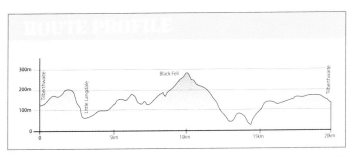

ROUTE PROFILE

**NEED TO KNOW**

**Start/Finish:** Tilberthwaite car park
**Grid ref:** NY 306 009; **Approx postcode:** LA21 8DJ
**Nearest town:** Ambleside
**Total distance:** 20km/12 miles
**Total ascent:** 780m
**Approx time:** 1-2hrs
**OS Map:** OL6 *The English Lakes South-eastern Area*
**Refreshments:** Bring sarnies for this one.
**Best time:** Well-drained, firm trails that will work all year round and not too exposed to the weather either. A great winter outing.
**Want more:** Leave this one as it is and ride **Route 7** for a harder tour of the area.
**Weekend away:** The best base for this one is **Coniston**, where it can be bundled with the two rides starting there (**11 & 13**) as well as possibly **10 & 12**.

# DUNNERDALE FELLS

## Medium 2-3 hrs

↑ 650m

14km/9 miles

*Quarry ruins near the Walna Scar Road*

**UNDULATING** · **TECHNICAL** · **SINGLETRACK** · **NAVIGATION**

MEDIUM

## IN BRIEF

It's often said that it's the areas away from the mountains that make the best mountain biking in the Lakes, and this little gem is a perfect example. The **Dunnerdale Fells** are modest, grassy hills tucked away in the very south west of the region. They contain some seriously top-notch riding. This is the shortest way of taking in the best of the trails; linking a couple of stiff climbs with some cracking downhill and some scintillating 'natural' singletrack. The big dipper down the **Lickle Valley** sets the tone, but it's the narrow ribbon from **Stephenson Ground** round to **Kiln Bank** that grabs most of the plaudits—'natural' riding at its very best. There's some awkward navigation in the middle section—testing in good visibility and plain awful in clag. But aside from this, it's about as good a short loop as you're ever going to ride.

# DUNNERDALE FELLS

Due west of **Coniston Water** and south of the **Hard Knott** and **Wrynose Passes**, the **Dunnerdale Fells** feel very different to the higher mountains of the national park, with grassy rather than rocky summits and unusually, no real lakes to speak of. This route is essentially a loop around the region's highpoint: **Caw** (529m).

# THE ROUTE   Start: **Seathwaite** car park (GR: SD 229 962)

**START**   Turn **L** onto the road and then bear **R** at a fork *(Coniston—Unfit For Cars)*. Turn **R** again onto the **Walna Scar Road** (waymarked) and then keep **SA** as the main track bears **L** over a bridge. Now continue steeply upwards for around 1km and go through a gate.

**2.** Turn **R** immediately beyond the gate and join a narrow track that passes quarry ruins. Immediately after the 2nd set of ruins, bear **L**, off the main track, onto a broad grassy climb (the main track becomes a footpath now).

**3.** This eventually becomes vague, where you need to keep **R**, with a boggy plateau to your **L**. You'll pick up a faint singletrack that improves and leads to a stream crossing. Cross then bear **L** onto a rough but clear track and follow this down the valley, where it gradually becomes excellent singletrack.

**4.** Stay with it as it drops and then

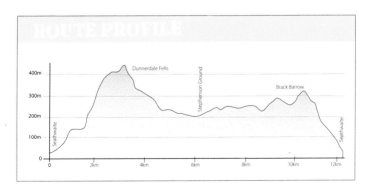

ROUTE PROFILE

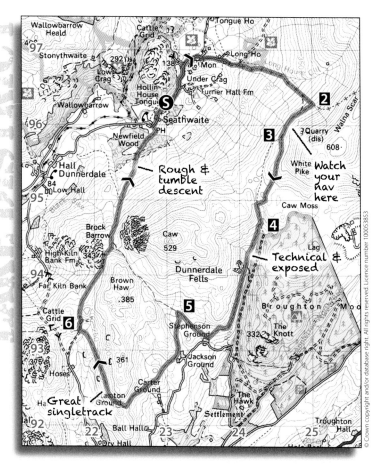

Labels visible on map: Wallowbarrow Heald, Cattle Grid, Tongue Ho, Stonythwaite, 292, 138, Mon, Long Ho, Low Crag, Under Crag, Turner Hall Fm, Hollin House Tongue, S, Seathwaite, Wallowbarrow, PH, Newfield Wood, 2, Quarry (dis), 608, Hall Dunnerdale, 84, Low Hall, Rough & tumble descent, 3, White Pike, Watch your nav here, Caw Moss, Brock Barrow, 343, High Kiln Bank Fm, Caw 529, 4, Lag, Technical & exposed, Far Kiln Bank, Dunnerdale Fells, Brown Haw .385, Broughton Moor, 94, 375, Cattle Grid, 6, 5, Stephenson Ground, 332, The Knott, Hoses, 361, Jackson Ground, Great singletrack, Carter Ground, anton Ground, The Hawk, Ha, al, 92, Ball Halls, Dry Hall, 22, 23, Settlement, 24, Troughton Hall, 25

climbs out of the valley before climbing and then dropping again slightly to a gate that leads onto the road. Don't go through but turn **R** to follow the wall. Keep **SA** with walls on both sides and eventually another gate ushers you onto open fell, where you drop, with the wall now on your **L**, onto a boggy plateau.

**5.** Bear **L** to cross the plateau and the beck, and then bear **L** again to pick up a clear track that runs uphill next to a wall. Now follow the main singletrack around the hillside for 3.5km, until you drop steeply to a major stream crossing and a x-roads with a good track.

**6.** Turn **R** onto this and climb steeply to a high path beneath **Goat Crag**. Keep **SA** to descend steeply and at the bottom, ignore a track to the **L** and keep **SA** to eventually curve **L** to the road. Turn **R** to finish.

## NEED TO KNOW

**Start/Finish:** Seathwaite Car Park
**Grid Ref:** SD 229 962; **Approx postcode:** LA20 6ED
**Nearest town:** Broughton-in-Furness
**Total distance:** 14km/9 miles
**Total ascent:** 650m
**Approx time:** 2-3hrs
**OS Map:** OL6 *The English Lakes South-western Area*
**Refreshments:** Bring sarnies for this one but the **Newfield Inn** at the start/finish is an excellent pub.

**Best time:** A better dry weather outing this one. The riding will be more fun and the ground is quite delicate in places.

**Want more:** The only obvious link-up is **Route 11**, which can be joined by keeping straight-ahead at **Point 2**. This'll make a classic Hard route.

**Weekend away:** The nearest really useful hub is **Coniston**, where **Routes 11 & 13** start. It's also good for **Route 12** and not bad for **9** or the **Grizedale loops (1 & 2)**.

# THE WALNA SCAR ROAD

**Hard** 4-5 hrs

↑ 850m

21km/12.5 miles

*Breathe easy on the summit*

**BIG UPS & DOWNS** · **TECHNICAL** · **MOUNTAIN** · **NAVIGATION**

*HARD*

## IN BRIEF

The **Walna Scar Road** is another of the infamous Lakes high passes and at over 600m at the highest point, it was once the highest highway in England too. This route takes over where **Route 10** leaves off and clambers its way right up to the pass in a do-able, but brutally challenging climb. The descent the other side used to be one of the best in Lakes and a real rite of passage for mountain bikers cutting their Lakeland teeth but some over-zealous path repairs have rendered it a little sterile at the time of writing, and it's now fast and furious rather than steep and technical. Hopefully a few harsh winters and plenty of summer rain will quickly return it to its former glory. The ride also takes in some excellent singletrack: first off in the woods on **Broughton Moor** and then in the wonderful **Lickle Valley**.

# WALNA SCAR ROAD

The **Walna Scar Road** was once a packhorse trail and a main trade route linking **Coniston** with the ports on the west coast. It has recently been in the news having been downgraded to a Restricted Byway after protracted discussions and appeals. The quarries, which are passed on this route and Route 10, were opened in the 1890s and closed in the early 1900s.

# THE ROUTE

**Start: Pay & display car park, Coniston** (GR: SD 303 976)

**START**   Turn **L** out of the car park and head into the village centre. Turn **L** onto the main road and cross the bridge before turning **L** again into **Lake Road**. Follow this down and as it swings **L** over the bridge, bear **R**, through a gate onto the Cycleway (*Torver*).

**2.** Follow the cycleway into the campsite and stay on the main drive, which is generally well-signed, and eventually leads up

*Above Torver*

to a road. Turn **R** to the A593 and then **L** into Torver. Continue out of the village and then take the first **R** to climb steeply towards Broughton. Continue to a forest gate on the **R**.

3. Go through and follow the fire road into the forest. Continue for just 300m and then look for an easily missed singletrack on the **R** (SD 254 930). Follow this across the valley to another fire road and keep **SA** onto a short, sweet singletrack descent. Drop to another fire road and turn **L** to cross a bridge.

4. Turn **L** again, then **R** onto another easy to miss singletrack. Follow this down to another fire road and turn **R** and then **L** to continue to the road. Turn **R** and climb up to some buildings.

5. Turn **R** though a gate and keep

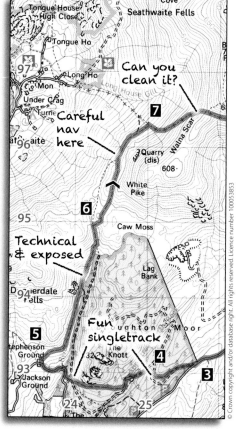

**R** to follow the wall up then down into the **Lickle Valley**. Enjoy fine singletrack above the stream continuing steeply upwards to open ground. The next section can be vague and quite difficult in poor visibility.

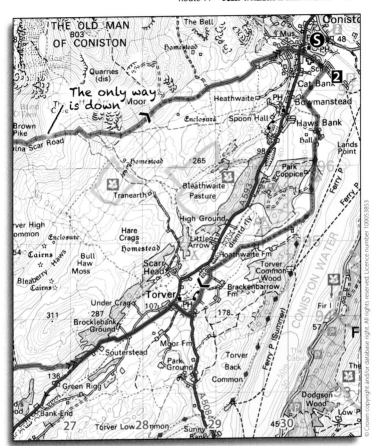

Continue to an obvious ford near **Dawson Pike**.

**6.** A vague track heads away from the ford. Follow this across a boggy plateau skirting around steep ground on the **L** and then the **R**, and climb to a pass.

Drop to quarry buildings and at the foot of these you'll rejoin a clear path that leads **R** to the **Walna Scar Road**.

**7.** Bear **R** and climb to the pass where you keep **SA** to descend for over 4km, crossing a

*The Walna Scar Road shows its teeth…*

bridge over **Torver Beck** and eventually reaching the end of the track in a large car parking area. Keep **SA** onto the road and drop to a junction where you fork **R** to the main road. Turn **L** back into **Coniston** and then **R** to the car park.

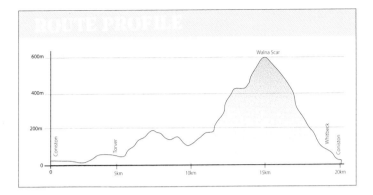

**Start/Finish:** Pay and Display Car Park, Coniston
**Grid ref:** SD 303 976; **Approx postcode:** LA21 8ET
**Nearest town:** Coniston
**Total distance:** 21km/12.5 miles
**Total ascent:** 850m
**Approx time:** 4-5hrs
**OS Map:** OL6 *The English Lakes South-western Area*

**Refreshments:** The **Church House Inn** at **Torver** is a great pub, but a bit early for a drink. The route can be started from here and they don't mind mountain bikers using their car park provided they pop in for a quickie after. Check first if possible.

**Best time:** Some delicate and soft ground makes this one a better dry weather outing.

**Want more:** Join **Route 13** at the bridge over **Torver Beck** and then follow this around the lake and back to **Coniston** for a tough figure-of-eight. Or join **Route 10** at **Point 5** and follow this around to Seathwaite and climb the whole pass, re-joining at **Point 7**.

**Weekend away:** The obvious partner ride is the **Round Coniston** route (**Route 13**) but a base around **Coniston** is also good for **Route 2** and isn't bad for **12** or even **9** & **10**.

# BLAWITH COMMON

## Route 12

**Easy** 2-3 hrs

↑ 520m

19km/12 miles

*Fast and flowing singletrack on the common*

EASY

## IN BRIEF

This loop feels about as far away from typical Lakeland riding as you'll ever get, yet it's an absolute belter with enough going on to keep riders of all levels happy. With a highpoint of just 183m, it's a classic example of how the best riding isn't always in the mountains; it is also good if the higher trails are clagged in, although the surfaces are delicate so it's no 'wet weather' outing. It starts on tarmac up to **Torver Low Common**, where a steep, loose crux provides the first real challenge. The gains are squandered quickly with a fast and furious run back down the other side. Another climb up through woodland and onto **Green Moor** and singletrack leads over from here: first up to **Woodland Fell** and then over **High Kep** to **Blawith**. An undulating road cruise provides brief respite before a stiff tarmac climb onto Torver Low Common, where top-notch trails take over and lead you past a lonely tarn.

EASY

# THE ROUTE Start: **Torver** car park (GR: SD 284 943)

**START** Head **SW** on the **A593** (towards Broughton) for 1km and take the first turning on the **L**. Follow it to the end and keep **SA** to follow a track around the edge of a field to a gate, where it becomes a clearer track. Climb over the pass and stay on the main track to drop to a road head. Keep **SA** for 1km to a waymarked **BW** on the **L**.

**2.** Follow this up, sticking to the main track, to an obvious but narrow trail on the **R**. Take this and then re-join the drive to **Green Moor Farm**. Keep **R** (farm to your **L**) to a gate and over a flagstone bridge. Bear **R** onto a narrow track and climb then traverse the hillside until you pass a rowan tree. Keep **SA** for 100m then bear sharp **L** onto a clear track.

**3.** Climb up to the pass and then follow the singletrack sweetly **SA** along the side of the hill. It becomes a walled track and leads to a drive. Turn **L** (effectively **SA**) and then keep **L** to drop to the **A5084**

*Easy climbing onto Blawith Common*

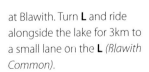

at Blawith. Turn **L** and ride alongside the lake for 3km to a small lane on the **L** (*Blawith Common*).

**4.** Follow this for over a km and then, immediately after a sharp **RH** bend, turn L onto a way-marked BW. Follow the track around the hillside and stay on the main track as it drops **L** into a dip. Stay with it over a couple of streams and then climb onto the ridge that runs alongside the lake. Keep **SA** to **Mill Bridge** and turn **L** onto a BW *(Torver)*. Follow this to a drive and turn **R** to the A5084. Turn **L** then **R** to finish.

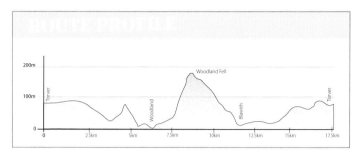

**Start/Finish:** Torver car park
**Grid ref:** SD 284 943; **Approx postcode:** LA21 8AZ
**Nearest town:** Coniston
**Total distance:** 19km/12 miles
**Total ascent:** 520m
**Approx time:** 2-3hrs
**OS Map:** OL6 *The English Lakes South-western Area*

**Refreshments:** Nothing on the route but the **Church House Inn** at **Torver** is perfect for a post ride pint. They don't mind mountain bikers using their car park as long as they go in for a pint afterwards. Always best to check.

**Best time:** Low enough to ride in bad weather but not a great winter ride as the trails are a bit too delicate. Seldom busy.

**Want more:** Link this one with **Route 13** by turning right at **Water Yeat**. This'll make a fairly tough tour of the lake .

**Weekend away:** The two **Coniston** starts aren't far (**Routes 11** & **13**) and **10** and even **9** isn't too bad.

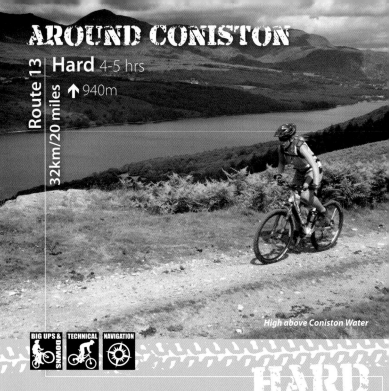

# AROUND CONISTON

**Hard** 4-5 hrs

↑940m

*High above Coniston Water*

BIG UPS & DOWNS  TECHNICAL  NAVIGATION

HARD

## IN BRIEF

There's something aesthetically pleasing about circumnavigating a large lake and **Coniston Water** is about perfect: exactly the right size and with great trails criss-crossing the hills on either side. There are many ways to skin this particular cat—from huge epics that fan out into the surrounding fells, to a short, sharp lap that uses tarmac to fill the gaps. This loop fits somewhere between: tough enough to satisfy most appetites; yet well within the reach of most riders. It starts on the **Walna Scar Road** (Routes 10 & 11) but this time it's tarmac that challenges not the trail. The drop into **Torver** is fun, it then combines with **Route 12** for some top-notch singletrack. The return leg sneaks around the southern tip of the lake and clambers up towards **Low Parkamoor** and **Grizedale Forest** (Route 2). It all ends with a full pelt descent to **Waterhead**, where easy road work gets you back into town..

# THE ROUTE

Start: Pay & display car park, **Coniston** (GR: SD 303 976)

**START**   Turn **L** out of the car park and ride into the village. Turn **L** onto the main road, and then immediately **R** up a narrow lane. Follow this past **The Sun Hotel** and turn sharp **R** at the top. Continue steeply uphill *(Walna Scar Road)* and this brings you to a gate and a car park.

**2.** Keep ahead to follow the main track, and ignore a steep track that climbs to the **R** after 1km. Continue for another 1km; and after a steep and narrow section turn **L** onto an easy-to-miss grassy track, just before **Torver Beck** (if you make the bridge you've gone too far).

**3.** Follow the grassy track down, past a disued quarry, and then through a stony chute to a bridge. Cross this and turn **L** onto a walled track. Keep **L** at a building and drop to **Scar Head Cottage**. Turn **L** and descend to the main road. Turn **R** into **Torver** and continue past the **A5094** for 1km, then take the first **L**—a narrow lane.

**4.** Follow this to its end at Haveriggholme and keep **SA**, through a gate, with a house up to the **L**. Keep **SA** to another gate and then climb steeply over a pass and drop down to join another road. Keep **SA** for

*High speed singletrack on Blawith Common*

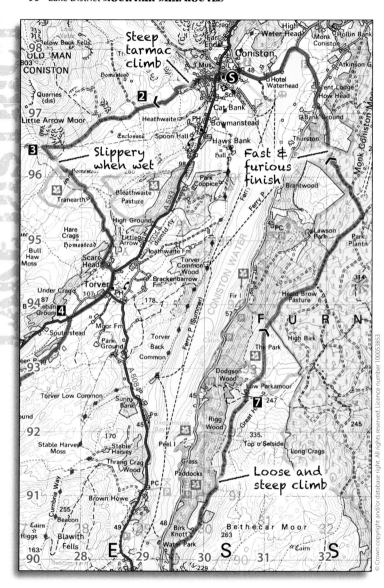

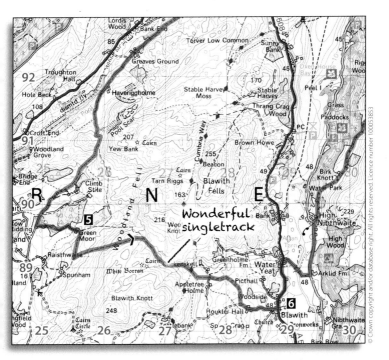

1km to a waymarked BW on the **L**. Follow this up to **Green Moor Farm**.

**5.** Keep **R**, with the farm to your **L**, to a gate and cross a flagstone bridge. Bear **R** onto a narrow track and climb then traverse until you pass a lone rowan tree. Keep **SA** for 100m and turn sharp **L** onto a clear track. Climb to a pass then follow singletrack **SA**. This becomes a walled track and leads to a drive that leads to the **A5084** at **Blawith**.

**6.** Turn **L** for 1km to **Water Yeats**, and turn **R** onto a narrow lane *(High Nibthwaite)*. Continue to a T-junction and turn **L** to **High Nibthwaite**. Turn **R**, through a gate, next to a telephone box, and swing immediately L. Continue for 5km to a junction at **Low Parkamoor**.

**7.** Drop **L** then climb past the house to join a good track.

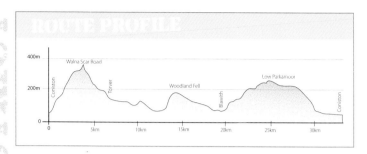

**ROUTE PROFILE**

**NEED TO KNOW**

**Start/Finish:** Pay & display car park, Coniston
**Grid Ref:** SD 303 976; **Approx postcode:** LA21 8ET
**Nearest town:** Coniston
**Total distance:** 34km/21 miles
**Total ascent:** 940m
**Approx time:** 4-5hrs
**OS Map:** OL6 *The English Lakes South-western Area*

**Refreshments:** The Church House Inn at Torver is a bit early really but note that they don't mind mountain bikers using their car park as long as they go in for a pint afterwards. Best to check. Plenty of choice in **Coniston**.

**Best time:** Some year-round trails but the drop to Torver and the section across the **Blawith Fells** won't stand up too well to wet weather.

**Want more:** Link up with Route 2 or The North Face trail as described in Route 2 (or both…).

**Weekend Away:** The obvious partner ride is the **Walna Scar route (Route 11)** but a base around here is also good for **Route 2** and isn't bad for **9** or even **10** & **12**.

Follow this for 3km to join a forest track. Turn **L** (effectively **SA**) for 1.1km to a crossroads. Bear **L** for 500m, and then turn **L** onto a BW. Follow this, keeping **SA** at the fork, and drop steeply on rough ground to the road. Turn **R** then **L** past **Waterhead** car park to the **B4285**. Turn **L** back into **Coniston**.

# BLACK COMBE

**Route 14**

**Easy** 2-3 hrs

↑ 640m

14km/9 miles

## BEST CLIMB

*Close to the summit of Black Fell*

## IN BRIEF

And now for something completely different. Closer to the coast than it is to the mountains, **Black Combe** certainly qualifies as Esoteria. But this is a cracker of a ride and well worth travelling the extra distance for. And it's also interesting to see a completely different side to the Lakes. This is a climber's route really: a one-up, one-down which kicks off with a huge pull all the way from sea level up to the 600m summit. The surfaces are reasonable and it's definitely do-able with commitment and stamina. But care's needed near the top not to blow the whole thing. The descent is fast and furious, with little to worry about apart from navigation and the odd sheep or walker you're likely to meet on the way. But you've worked hard to gain those 600m, so don't give them up too easily. Take your time and enjoy.

EASY

# BLACK COMBE

Although it's only 600m high, low by Lakeland standards, **Black Combe** is tucked away on the coast, over ten kilometres from any higher ground, so it's an amazing viewpoint. As well as the majority of the Lakeland Peaks to the east, it's also possible to see Wales and even the Isle of Man from its summit.

## THE ROUTE

Start: Lay-by 200m south of **Whitbeck** (GR: SD 120 837)

**START**   Head south down the A595 to Whicham and bear **L** (Broughton), still on the A595. Continue for 500m to a narrow lane on the **L** and take this, climbing up past a house at the top and onto dirt. Continue to a junction by a gate and turn **R**.

Now stay on the main track to climb for just over 3km to the summit.

**2.** Careful navigation needed here. Head north on a vague track that improves after the first drop. You're aiming to stay close

*Nearly there... great views back over the sea*

to the ridge top, which veers north-west. Don't be tempted too far **L**—wrong valley altogether—or to the **R**, which is definitely off-line. As the track improves so it swings west then north-west again and then south-west.

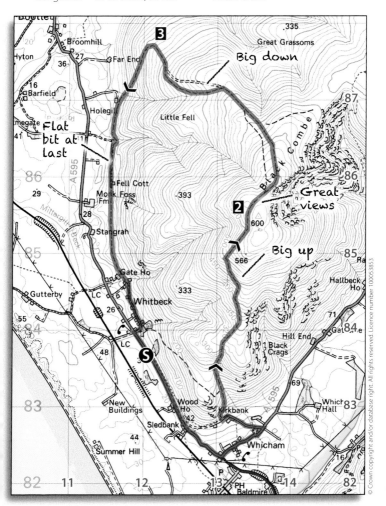

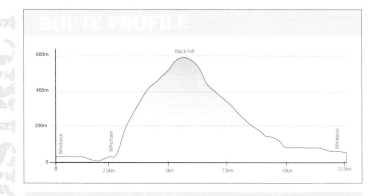

Black Fell

Whitbeck    Whicham    Whitbeck

**Start/Finish:** Lay-by on A595, 200m south of Whitbeck

**Grid ref:** SD 120 837; **Approx postcode:** LA19 5UR

**Nearest town:** Broughton-in-Furness

**Total distance:** 14km/9 miles

**Total ascent:** 640m

**Approx time:** 2-3hrs

**OS Map:** OL6 *The English Lakes South-western Area*

**Refreshments:** Take sarnies—there's nothing on the way round. The **Miners Arms** in **Silecroft** is perfectly placed for a pint afterwards.

**Best time:** Avoid bad weather; the summit's no place to be on a windy day and navigation would be awkward in poor visibility. The trails will work when wet though.

**Want more:**  You're out on a limb here. Best to pack up and head for **Eskdale** (**Route 15**) or one of the **Coniston** area routes.

**Weekend away:** This one can be included into any weekend in the South West lakes.

**3.** The track then bends sharp **L** ahead of a wall. Keep the wall to your **R** and follow the obvious track south around the hillside until it eventually leads to houses at **Whitbeck Mill**. Follow the drive down to the main road and turn L back to the lay-by.

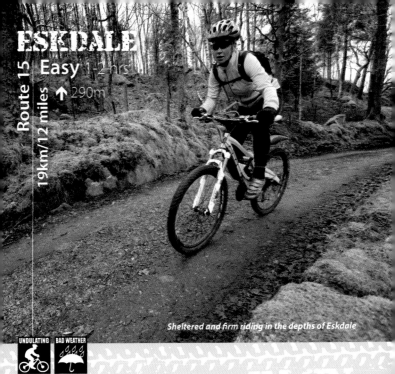

# ESKDALE
## Easy 1-2 hrs
↑ 290m

UNDULATING  BAD WEATHER

*Sheltered and firm riding in the depths of Eskdale*

EASY

## IN BRIEF

This is the easiest route in the book, despite the distance. But it's a fun little outing, set among some wonderful scenery. It's well sheltered and on good surfaces thoughout; making it perfect for those days that you really don't want to be in the mountains. And it's also ideal for less experienced or younger mountain bikers. There's even a good pub on the way round and another near the finish. The outward leg is split between tarmac and a well-surfaced forest track—an easy warm-up if ever there was one; and the opening section of the return leg won't pose any problems either. But the final stretch of the **Esk Trail**, from **Forge Bridge** to **Low Birker**, is varied, fun and packed with plenty of little surprises. You'll be grinning at the end.

EASY

# ESKDALE

Famous for being one of just a few major Lakeland valleys that don't have their own lake, **Eskdale** is a stunning and relatively secluded glen tucked away in the far west of the National Park. It's protected by imposing fells to the north, south and east, and is easiest reached via **Ravensglass**, where the **River Esk** finally empties into the sea.

## THE ROUTE Start: **Dalesgarth Station** (GR: NY 173 007)

**START** Turn **R** onto the road and follow it for 2km to a T-junction at **Eskdale Green**. Turn **L** *(Ulpha)*, cross **Forge Bridge** and then continue around a **LH** bend before turning **R** onto a

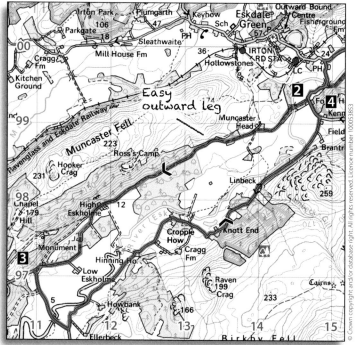

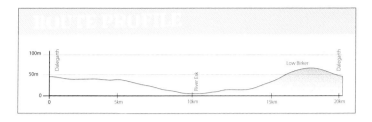

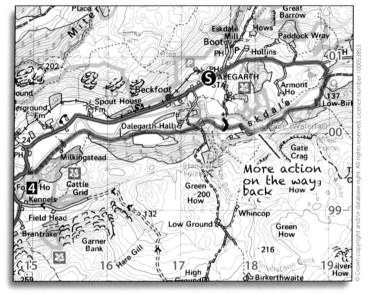

waymarked track (*Eskdale Trail, Muncaster Castle*), by a large barn.

**2.** Follow this broad forest track for 4km to a signed fork immediately after **High Eskholme**. Turn **L**, drop to a gate and then follow way-marks over the golf course to the edge of the wood, where you turn **R** to follow singletrack to a gate. Go through and follow the track to a T-junction where you turn R and continue out onto the A595.

**3.** Turn **L** and cross Muncaster Bridge before turning **L** onto a lane. Follow this for over 5km to a T-junction and turn **L** (*Eskdale*

*Green, Whitehaven)* to ride past the turning you took earlier. Continue to a BW on the **R** before the bridge. Take this and follow it alongside the **River Esk**.

**4.** Stay on this for 2.5km and keep **SA** at a x-roads to a ford and bridge. Climb away, keeping slightly right after the gate, and continue to a junction with a gate ahead, where you keep **R** to stay above the wall. Continue to **Low Birker Farm** and turn **L** to drop past the farm and down to a bridge. Turn **L** over the bridge and continue to a T-junction, where you turn **L** to finish.

## NEED TO KNOW

**Start/Finish:** Dalesgarth Station
**Grid Ref:** SD 173 007; **Approx postcode:** CA19 1TG
**Nearest town:** Egremont
**Total Distance:** 21km/13 miles
**Total ascent:** 290m
**Approx time:** 1-2hrs
**OS Map:** OL6 *The English Lakes South-western Area*
**Refreshments:** King George IV in Eskdale Green but this is perhaps too early for the way out so re-cross **Forge Bridge** later on. Or the **Woolpack** at Eskdale.
**Best time:** A year round route that's ideal for a bad day. Popular with walkers though.
**Want more:** With a bit of careful map reading and some real determination you can follow the bridleway that leads east from **Eskdale Green** up **Miterdale** to **Burnmoor Tarn**, where you can return via a very vague track that becomes a great descent as it nears **Boot**. Note: a lot of untracked ground—some boggy. You need to be keen.
**Weekend away:** Like **Black Combe**, this one's tucked away a bit so rather than basing yourself around here, use one of the usual hubs and pop out for a different day.

*Remote riding in Bowderdale*

### Ullswater & the Central Fells

### Howgill Fells

### Around Keswick

# THE NORTH

# HELVELLYN

## Hard 4-5 hrs

↑ 360m

26km/16 miles

*Between Helvellyn and White Side*

HARD

## IN BRIEF

**Helvelyn** is about as high as you can legally ride in England, and it's only a few metres short of the highest point in the country altogether, so it's definitely safe to describe this one as a **full-on mountain route**. But having said that, the climb up is predominantly do-able—only a couple of short, sharp push/carry sections—and the main descent from **Whiteside** has recently been resurfaced and is ride-able by just about anyone with decent brakes. But this is more than just a ride; it's a full-on adventure that's well worth preparing properly for and saving for a good day. You'll enjoy the riding for sure, but the biggest buzz will come just from having crossed such dramatic terrain on your bike. Only problem is, big rides like this can become addictive.

# HELVELLYN

At 950m, **Helvellyn** is England's third highest peak and a much sought-after tick for hill walkers. It's not so much a separate summit as a high point on a north-south ridge that runs from **Threlkeld** in the north to **Rydal** in the south, dividing the **Thirlmere** and **Patterdale valleys**. It's at its most dramatic from the east where it's propped up by the two distinctive knife-edge arêtes of Striding Edge and Swirral Edge.

## THE ROUTE (Start: **Glenridding** car park (GR: NY 385 169)

**START** Turn **L** onto the road and enjoy an easy warm-up until you reach the A5091. Turn **L** onto this and climb steeply into **Dockray**. Turn **L** at the **Royal Hotel** and continue up for another 1.5km to a x-roads. Here, keep **SA**, onto a track that leads to a ford over **Groove Beck**.

**2.** Cross then turn immediately **L** onto a faint track which quickly establishes itself. Stay on this for over 2km keeping **SA** wherever it becomes faint. It eventually swings left and climbs steeply over **Matterdale Common**. Keep the first summit to your **L** and drop briefly before climbing again to the summit of **Great Dodd**.

*On the climb to Raise with Stybarrow Dodd in the distance*

*Dropping back towards Glenridding*

**3.** Keep **SA** (vague) and aim at a clear track on the ridge ahead. Once on this, keep the escarpment to your left and continue beneath **Watson's Dodd** and then up towards **Stybarrow Dodd**. Drop and then climb up to **Raise**—the final few metres are a carry—then follow the clear track on the far side and drop into the saddle beneath **White Side**.

**4.** For **Helvellyn's summit**, keep **SA** again, over **White Side** and down into the next col from where a steep climb leads onto the main ridge. Turn **L** to drop slightly then climb to the summit itself. To descend, retrace your tracks back to points 4/5. (The route can be shortened by 1-1.5hrs

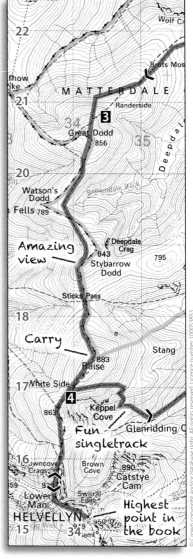

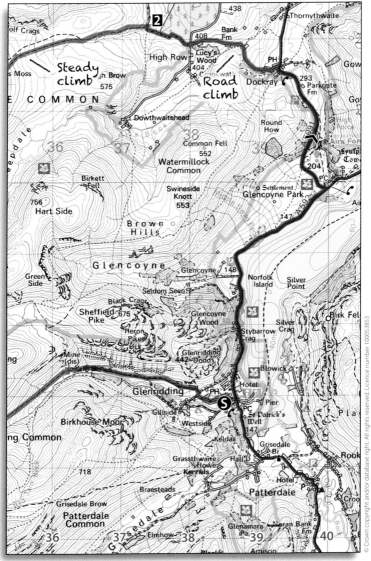

*Approaching the summit of Helvellyn from the saddle beneath Lower Man*

by missing out this section and continuing as 5).

**5.** Once back beneath **White Side**, take the narrow track **R** (**L** for short cut), and follow this down, around a number of switchbacks until it becomes a broad stony track that leads down to the **YHA**. Keep **SA** here to join the road that will drop you back into **Glenridding**.

## NEED TO KNOW

**Start/Finish:** Car park, Glenridding

**Grid Ref:** NY 385 169; **Approx postcode:** CA11 0PZ

**Nearest town:** Keswick

**Total distance:** 26km/16 miles

**Total ascent:** 1360m

**Approx time:** 4-5 hrs

**OS Map:** OL5 *The English Lakes North-eastern Area*

**Refreshments:** Dockwray's a bit early so take sarnies. Choice of cafés plus the Traveller's Rest in **Glenridding** when you finish.

**Best time:** The summit is exposed to everything that's going—choose a good day. And the main climb up is too soft to consider after prolonged wet weather. Popular with walkers so best to avoid peak season.

**Want more:** Continue south over **Nethermost Pike** and Dollywagon Pike and descend to **Grisedale Tarn**, where you can follow **Grisedale** back. This is seriously full-on and wil involve some big carries—both up and down.

**Weekend away:** A Patterdale/Glenridding base will give easy access to **Route 17** and **Route 18** and won't be too far from the **Keswick loops (Routes 20, 21 & 22)** either.

# HIGH STREET

**Ride 17**

**Epic** 5-7 hrs

↑ 1300m

35km/22 miles

*Ullswater singletrack on a winter's evening*

BIG UPS & BOMBS · TECHNICAL · MOUNTAIN · NAVIGATION · PUSH OR CARRY

EPIC

## IN BRIEF

**High Street** has long been a rite of passage for Lakeland mountain bikers, and rightly so: rideable trails at 800m above sea level aren't two a penny in England. But the real highlights of this Epic come after the highpoint has been crossed: first on some great singletrack that contours around **Loadpot Hill** and then drops down towards the shores of **Ullswater**—the views are as good as the riding but you'll have to stop to admire them. And then on the ever-popular rocky horror show that is the trail that runs alongside the lake (avoid at busy times). The climbing's murder: no point in denying it. But after a tortuous start, this route just gets better and better. Shame it's so tough; otherwise it would be worth a second lap.

# HIGH STREET

If you've ever asked what the Romans ever did for mountain biking, here's an answer. It's amazing that their dedication to the straight meant they chose the felltops at over 800m above sea level rather than the sheltered valleys. But then again, we're grateful for the trail—thanks guys. **High Street** is also the name of a fell (828m), just south of, but reachable from this loop, which was named after the road that crosses it.

## THE ROUTE Start: **Patterdale** car park (GR: NY 398 158)

**START** Turn **L** onto the **A592** and follow it for 1.9km to **Deepdale Bridge** where you turn **L** onto a BW. Cross two fields to join a farm track that drops to a stream. Cross and veer **L** to join a good track. Turn **R** and follow this to a ford. Cross and keep **SA** on a stony track that leads to the road at **Hartsop**.

**2.** Turn **L** and go through the hamlet to a car park. Keep **SA**, on a good track, and follow it down to the river, keeping **R** at a fork. Climb away and continue SA to **Hayeswater**. Turn **L** near the outflow and climb steeply up the grassy hillside on a zigzag track. Turn **R** on the ridge and follow the track around the **L** of **The Knott**.

**3.** This veers **R** and drops to a T-junction by a wall. Turn **L** and climb to **Rampsgill Head**.

*On the flanks of Barton Fell with Ullswater far below*

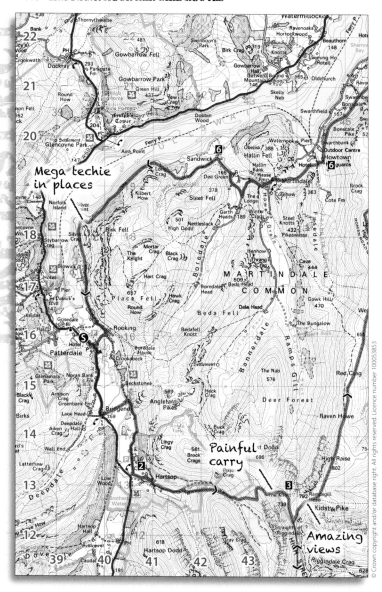

Mega techie in places

Painful carry

Amazing views

Where it levels, fork **L** onto a very faint track that continues to **High Raise**. Keep **SA**, following the main track for 4km to a fork by a large cairn beneath **Loadpot Hill**.

**4.** Fork **L** and traverse around the hill before dropping steeply for a short distance. The track then veers right and levels before dropping steadily for another 4km, ignoring a junction on the **L** to **Arthur's Pike**. Continue beneath **Heughscar Hill** to a junction with a clear path close to the **Cockpit**.

**5.** Turn sharp **L** onto this and traverse the hillside, drop into a ravine and then climb to a x-roads, where you keep **SA**. Drop to the wall and then continue along it (ignoring two obvious paths to the right), to a gate between houses at **Mellguard**. Ride down the drive, past the houses; then turn **L**, through a gate, to a footbridge.

**6.** Cross and keep **SA** to climb then traverse the hillside. Continue for 1km and fork **R** to the road, by a small church. Turn **L** onto the road and then keep **R** (*Sandwick*) to drop to

*Stony singletrack on the shores of Ullswater*

a bridge. Climb away and bear **L** to a T-junction. Turn sharp **R** for 1km to a BW on the **L** (*Patterdale*).

**7.** Follow this up and then along the side of the lake for a few kms until it eventually goes through a gate and becomes a broad track. Keep **SA** past Side Farm to a gate that gives access to the road. Follow this **R** and down to the **A592**, where you turn **R** to finish.

## NEED TO KNOW

**Start/Finish:** Patterdale car park
**Grid ref:** NY 398 158; **Approx postcode:** CA11 0NW
**Nearest town:** Keswick
**Total distance:** 35km/22 miles
**Total ascent:** 1300m
**Approx time:** 5-7hrs
**OS Map:** OL6 *The English Lakes North-eastern Area*

**Refreshments:** Take sarnies although there's a tea room in **Side Farm** near the end, in the summer. **The White Lion** in **Patterdale** is handy at the end.

**Best time:** A bit high and exposed for a winter route so stick to milder months but avoid peak season and school holidays like the plague or time your ride carefully—eg. finish late.

**Want more:** Unlikely but climb **High Street** itself—south from **Point 3**—if you really need to.

**Weekend away:** A Patterdale/Glenridding base will give easy access to **Route 16** and **Route 18** and isn't too far from the **Keswick loops** (**Routes 20, 21 & 22**) either.

## ROUTE PROFILE

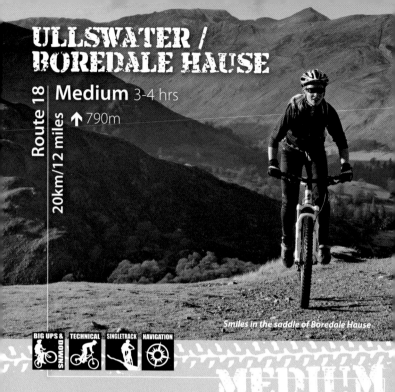

# ULLSWATER / BOREDALE HAUSE

## Medium 3-4 hrs

↑790m

*Smiles in the saddle of Boredale Hause*

**BIG UPS & DOWNS** · **TECHNICAL** · **SINGLETRACK** · **NAVIGATION**

**MEDIUM**

## IN BRIEF

A classic loop that manages to cram a little of everything that's mind-blowing about Lakeland mountain biking into a measly 20km. The climbs are big and steep but totally ride-able. Well, 99.9% anyway—you'll probably push a little on the singletrack onto **Beda Fell** and maybe one or two of the steep, rocky ramps around Ullswater too. And the descents are among the finest in the book: arm-achingly long and semi-techie from **Beda Fell**—line choice and commitment are everything; and short but seriously sharp alongside Ullswater—clean this lot and you can consider yourself half-tasty. Make sure you time your attack well though, or there'll be a family of dog walkers in the way just when you don't need them. It's also a tough outing, with nearly 800m of ascent making it perhaps the most brutal of Mediums in the book. Allow plenty of time and enjoy….

# ULLSWATER

Almost 9 miles long and a mile across at its widest point, **Ullswater** is Lakeland's second largest lake and far more scenic than its larger sibling, Windermere, with impressive mountains crowding it in on all sides. It's a typical 'ribbon' lake, left behind by retreating glaciers at the end of the last Ice Age, and is over 60m deep in places.

# THE ROUTE   Start: **Brothers Water** car park (GR: NY 402 134)

**START**   Turn **R** out of the car park onto the A592 and then **L** to **Hartsop**. Take the 1st **L** and continue past the holiday park and along a stony lane to a gate and ford. Now bear **L** onto a good track and follow it for 1.5km to a steep ramp on the **R**. Climb steeply all the way up to a plateau at **Boredale Hause**.

**2.** Keep **R**, but not onto the very narrow, rough stony footpath that climbs onto the peak above. The track is grassy to start with and bears **R** to cross a couple of rocky knolls. It then

*Committing to the drop from Beda Fell*

improves and drops to **Freeze Beck**, before climbing onto the ridge of **Beda Fell**. Continue to a large cairn.

**3.** Turn **R** to drop off of the ridge (don't continue along the ridge) and then bear **L** to drop down the hillside to the farm at **Dale Head**. Go through the farmyard, and continue past a small church to a triangle, where you turn **L** to drop to a junction. Turn **R** to a bridge and then climb to a BW on the **L** *(Patterdale)*.

**4.** Follow this up and then along the side of the lake for a few kms until it eventually goes through a gate and becomes a broad track. Keep **SA** past **Side Farm** to a gate that gives access to the road. Follow this **R** and down to the A592, where you turn **L** to finish.

*High on Beda Fell*

**4**

Watermook
Obelisk 388
Hallin Fell
ne Park
Aira Point
Ferry
Sandwick
Doe Green
165
Hallin
Bank
Hause
Fm
Martí
19
Cotehow
Long
Crag
147
Silver
Point
Kilbert
How
Sleet Fell
378
The
Lodge
Winter
Crags
189
Steel
Knotts
432
18
Birk Fell
501
High Dodd
Nettleslack
Garth
Heads
Silver
Crag

Mega techie
in places
Knight
Crag
Black
Crag
Henhow
Thrang
Crag
M A R T I N D
Hart Crag
Boredale
Boredale Beck
Staybrow Beck
Waterfall
Boredale
Head
Boredald
Head
509
Beda Head
C O M M O
17
657
Place Fell
Hawk
Crag
Singletrack
descent
Dale Head
ck's
Round
How
B e d a   F e l l
Careful nav
**2**
Rooking
16
Bannerdale Beck
**3**
Settlement
The Nab
576
Hotel
rdale
Boredale
Hause
Crookabeck
15
Steep but
rideable
Heck
Crag
Deer Fo
oran Bank
Fm
Backstones
Angletarn
Pikes
enbank Fm
e Head
pdale
Hall
Bridgend
159
Angle
Tarn
Buck
Crag
Satura
Crag
Rest Dodd
696
14
Lingy
Crag
561
Brock
Crags
**S**
Prison
Crag
Low
40
13
41
Hartsop
42
43
13

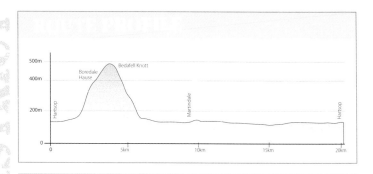

**Start/Finish:** Brothers Water car park
**Grid Ref:** NY 402 134; **Approx postcode:** CA11 0NZ
**Nearest town:** Ambleside
**Total distance:** 20km/12 miles
**Total ascent:** 790m
**Approx time:** 3-4hrs
**OS Map:** OL6 *The English Lakes South-eastern Area*

**Refreshments:** Take sarnies although there's a tea room in Side Farm near the end, in the summer. The **White Lion** in **Patterdale** is close enough for a drink afterwards.

**Best time:** The trail alongside **Ullswater** is narrow and very popular with walkers—for maximum enjoyment avoid peak season weekends or go early or late. **Boredale Hause** can be wet and exposed but the rest of the route will go in any conditions really.

**Want more:** From **Martindale**, head north east on the road to **Pooley Bridge** and then climb up to the **Cockpit** (NY 482 222) to follow **Route 17** to finish.

**Weekend away:** A **Patterdale/Glenridding** base will give easy access to **Route 16** & **17** and isn't too far from the **Keswick loops** (**Routes 20, 21** & **22**).

# THE HOWGILL FELLS

Route 19

52km/31 miles

**Epic** 5-7 hrs

↑ 1600m

BEST
SINGLETRACK

TOP
FIVE

*Great riding at over 600m on The Calf*

| BIG UPS & DOWNS | TECHNICAL | MOUNTAIN | NAVIGATION | PUSH OR CARRY | SINGLETRACK |

EPIC

## IN BRIEF

**Bowderdale** is the finest stretch of singletrack in the book and one of the best in the country. But it comes at a price and this loop makes you earn every last inch of the mind-blowing 6km ribbon of red dirt, notching up a respectable 52km . First up, an explanation: the route doesn't actually enter the Lake District National Park at all, but sneaks briefly into the Yorkshire Dales National Park at one point, so what's it doing here? Ride it, then ask how we could have left it out. It makes a perfect outing when the mountains further west are just too busy. It's a three-up, three-down; although the first two ups and downs pale into insignificance in comparison to the third, which is a brutal push/carry/struggle onto **The Calf**. But it'll be the ecstasy of **Bowderdale** that you'll remember when it's all over. Well, this plus the breath-taking scenery and gargantuan views that accompany it.

# THE ROUTE Start: **Orton** car park (GR: NY 622 082)

**START** Head uphill from the car park and bear **L** onto the **B6261**. Follow this for 500m and take the 1st **L** *(Greenholme)*. At **Greenholme**, go past a farm and turn **L** *(Tebay, Kendal)*, then cross the bridge over **Bretherdale Beck** before turning **R** to ride up the dale.

**2.** Continue **SA** at a T-junction to cross the bridge then bear **R**. Then, after 1km, turn **L** onto a stony track *(Public Byway Breasthigh Road)* and climb steeply to the top. Keep **SA** to descend steeply to the banks of **Borrow Beck**.

**3.** Cross the stepping stones and join a good track, where you turn **L** to ride down the dale, crossing a bridge after 1.5km.

Keep below derelict buildings at **High Borrowdale** and bear **R**, into the yard at **Low Borrowdale**.

**4.** Continue down, eventually crossing another bridge and continuing above a campsite.

After a short, sharp climb, turn right (easily missed—if you reach the cattle grid, you've gone past it) onto a vague track that climbs steeply up to join a better track. Then climb steeply on a clear grassy track that eventually joins a drive by the mast.

**5.** Turn **R** and follow the drive downhill for 3km, turning **L** onto the lane at the bottom and following it to the **A685**. Turn **L** for 1.2km and then

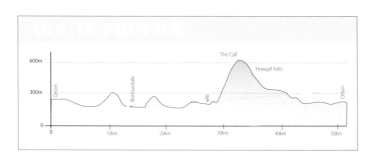

*Dropping into Bowderdale on sweet singletrack*

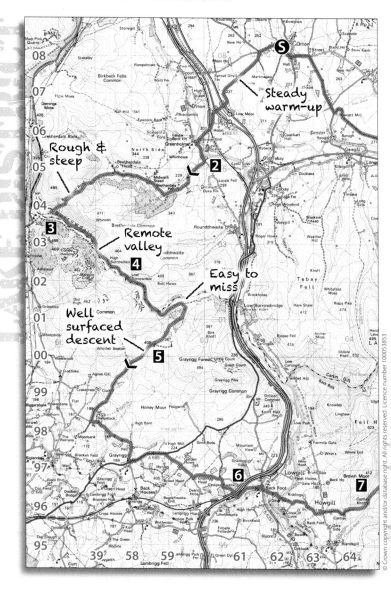

**S**

Steady warm-up

Rough & steep

**2**

Remote valley

**3**

**4**

Easy to miss

Well surfaced descent

**5**

**6**

**7**

*Winding down Bowderdale*

turn **R** *(Lambrigg)*. Turn **L** after 1km *(Lowgill)* and after crossing the motorway, turn L (Beckfoot and Tebay).

**6.** Turn **R** and immediately **L**, beneath the viaduct, and cross the bridge to continue up the road to a x-roads, where you go **SA**. Keep L at the farm at **Castley** and drop down to **Chapel Beck**. Cross and take the grassy track that climbs steeply up the side of the mountain.

**7.** Swing right at the top, towards the summit, and then bear **L**, just short of it, to traverse beneath it. Turn **L** onto another track and then

## NEED TO KNOW

**Start/Finish:** Orton car park
**Grid ref:** NY 318 256; **Approx postcode:** CA10 3RU
**Nearest town:** Orton
**Total distance:** 52km/31 miles
**Total ascent:** 1600m
**Approx time:** 5-7 hrs
**OS Map:** OL19 *Howgill Fells & Upper Eden Valley and OL7 English Lakes South-eastern areas.*

**Refreshments:** Take sarnies for the ride—lots of them—but the **George Hotel** or the **Village Tea Shop** in **Orton** are perfect for recovery.

**Best time:** A better summer route really: the fell tops are just too exposed in bad weather and the **Bowderdale** singletrack is too precious and delicate to destroy during really wet periods.

**Want more:** Unlikley….

**Weekend away:** If you fancy a second outing, explore the trails to the east of **Horton** over **Great Ashby Scar**, or head across to the **Staveley/Ings** area (**Routes 4, 5 & 6**).

keep **R**, with a pool on your **L**, to follow a broad track with drainage gullies. This becomes singletrack that you follow for 7km, eventually meeting a 4x4 track coming in from the **L**.

8. Follow the wall down to a gate and continue on a clear track through a couple of fields to the road. Turn **R** to drop to go under the **A685** and turn **L** at a T-junction after 300m. Turn **R** as you leave **Kelleth** *(Orton)* and then **L** onto a track *(Fawcett Mill)*. At the end turn **R** onto the **B6261** and follow it to **Orton** to finish.

# BORROWDALE CLASSIC

Route 20

**Hard** 4-5 hrs

↑940m

28km/18 miles

*Great singletrack high above Borrowdale*

UNDULATING  TECHNICAL  BAD WEATHER

## IN BRIEF

This is such an unlikely classic. It's that exceptional track by a band that you usually don't enjoy. Why? Loads of tarmac and an almost un-rideable man-made trail should go some way to explaining it. But despite this, it really is a classic and it's also one of the best and most technical loops in this book. In all fairness the worst of the road comes at the beginning: a perfect and scenic warm-up beside the lovely **Derwent Water** followed by a stiff pull up past the iconic **Ashness Bridge**. A rough and rubble-strewn trail helps you hurdle the hilltop above **Watendlath** and then just as you begin to enjoy yourself, you fall foul of someone's idea of drainage gullies—ravines might be a better word. But from herein it's just superb. Fast and furious, down past **Castle Crag**, and then panoramic beyond belief around **Cat Bells**. It finishes where it started: on the asphalt, but odds are you'll be smiling all the way to the end.

Road warm-up

Great views

Ashness Fell

# BORROWDALE

Linked to Buttermere via the Honister Pass and draining into Derwent Water to the north, **Borrowdale** nestles deep in the heart of the Lake District and has a wonderfully remote feel. This is actually one of two Borrowdales featured in this book: the other is visited on **Route 19**.

# THE ROUTE

Start: Otley Road car park, **Keswick** (GR: NY 266 235)

**START**  Turn **R** onto the main road, follow this down to **Main Street** and turn **R** to the junction with **Heads Rd**. Turn **L** into this, and follow it around to a roundabout. Turn **R** towards **Borrowdale** and continue for 2.5km to a **L** fork (*Watendlath*). Take this to the road end at **Watendlath**, and turn **R** over the bridge.

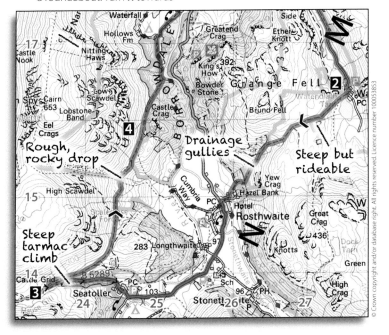

*Fast and furious on the drop to Castle Crag*

**2.** Fork immediately **R** onto a stony BW and climb then drop into **Borrowdale**—keeping **R** through a gate at halfway. Keep **SA** on tarmac into **Rosthwaite** and turn **L** to **Seatoller**. Continue up towards the **Honister Pass** for 1.2km, where you cross a cattle grid. Locate a BW running parallel to the road on the **R** and as the road turns **L**, turn sharp **R** onto it.

**3.** Continue through a gate, and then, after 400m, as you approach a copse on your **R**, fork **L** (easy to miss) onto a singletrack BW (waymark on the **L**). Climb to a gate and keep **SA** on undulating singletrack, crossing a couple more becks, before dropping steeply beside **Castle Crag**.

**4.** Keep **SA** into the wood, and bear **L** at the water to follow a drive to a T-junction with a road. Bear **R** into **Grange** and turn **L** in the village and then **L** again, after 1.2km (marked a footpath but turns immediately into a BW). Climb steeply on a rough track and then fork **R** at the top onto a singletrack BW that follows the wall.

**5.** Continue around the hill and down to the road. Turn **L** and immediately **L** again, to follow another BW around the hillside. Drop to the road again and turn **L** and then **R**, down a steep hill. Turn **R** at the next junction and follow the road into **Portinscale**. Turn **R** *(Keswick)* to cross the river to the B5288 and turn **R** to finish.

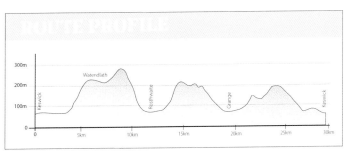

ROUTE PROFILE

**Start/Finish:** Otley Road car park, Keswick
**Grid ref:** NY 266 235; **Approx postcode:** CA12 5JL
**Nearest town:** Keswick
**Total distance:** 28km/18 miles
**Total ascent:** 940m
**Approx time:** 4-5 hrs
**OS Map:** OL5 *The English Lakes North-eastern Area*
**Refreshments:** Tea shops in **Watendlath, Rosthwaite** and **Seatoller**, but the best bet is **Grange**, near the end. Pubs in Roswaithe and Seatoller. Pedlar Café in **Keswick** at the end too.
**Best time:** Great, rocky, year-round trails. Some sections are very busy with walkers.
**Want more:** No obvious extension here. Have lunch then head north on Lonscale Fell (Route 22).
**Weekend away:** With **Keswick** as a base, you're in easy reach of **Route 21** and **Route 22**, and not so far from **16, 17 & 18**. That's a week's worth.

# BACK o' SKIDDAW

**Route 21**

**Hard** 3-4 hrs

↑ 950m

32km/20 miles

*Climbing up to Whitewater Dash*

UNDULATING  BAD WEATHER

HARD

## IN BRIEF

This one could be seen as the perfect partner for **Route 22**; making it into a huge tour of the area. But the character of the riding's so different, it seemed appropriate to split them and let both stand on their own. It's a brilliant outing that crosses some fairly remote territory in the far north of the National Park. The outward leg follows rough mining tracks that until relatively recently were out of bounds to bikes, and they are great fun to ride, even if they don't throw up too many challenges. The real test piece comes on the clamber up the side of **Whitewater Dash**—this used to be a lot rougher but is still a challenge even with a decent surface. This is rewarded with a full pelt blast down to the infant **River Caldew**—a great splash on a hot day. The drop from **Skiddaw House** is just plain good fun, with some great, well-surfaced sections and the odd peaty trap to break the flow.

HARD

## SKIDDAW

At 931m, **Skiddaw** is the 4th highest peak in England and pushes **Helvellyn** hard for the highest trail in the book (see extension suggestion **Route 22**). **Back o' Skiddaw**, is a local term for the area crossed by this ride.

## THE ROUTE  Start: **Mosedale Bridge** (GR: NY 357 322)

**START**   Head into **Mosedale** village and keep **SA** past the telephone box to head out onto open ground. Bear **L** after 3km, and at the top of the hill, immediately before farm buildings on your **R**, bear **L** onto a waymarked permissive BW.

**2.** Go through the barrier and follow the main track around the hillside to some mine workings. Keep **L** to stay on the main track and climb steeply

for a short distance, then turn **R** to traverse again, still on the main track. Drop into a valley and bear round to the **L** to climb out again.

**3.** Continue for another 1km to a T-junction with a grassy trail and turn **R** onto it. Drop to cross a stream and then continue down to 'T' into a gravel track by a wall. Turn **R** and then **L**, through a gate, to drop to the road at **Fell Side**.

*Near Skiddaw House*

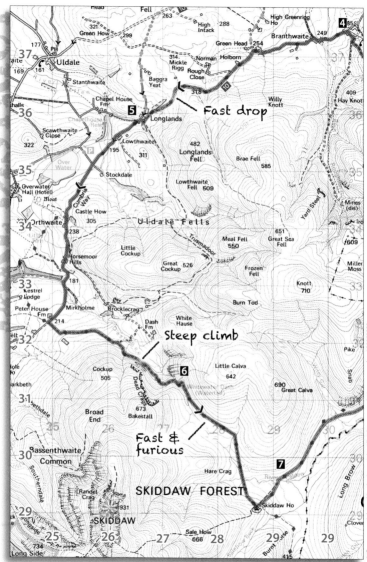

Fast drop

Steep climb

Fast & furious

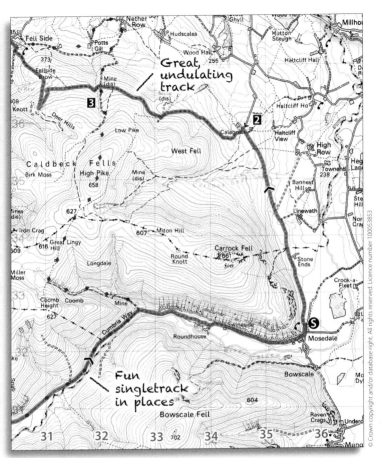

**4.** Turn **L** and follow the road for 2km to **Green Head**, where you turn **L** onto a tarmac drive that crosses a white bridge before it becomes rougher after passing a farm on the **R**. Keep **SA** at the next fork (another farm drive) and then continue over a ford and down to the road at **Longlands**.

**5.** Turn **L** for 3km to a junction with a turning on the **R**. Don't take this but cross **Cassbeck Bridge** and turn **L** onto a

*Easy going on the Caldbeck Fells*

waymarked BW. Go through the gate and **SA** on the main track. When it starts to drop, bear **R** to climb up past **Whitewater Dash** waterfall.

**6.** Cross the beck and follow the zigzag up to the top. Descend to cross **Dead Beck**, and then climb back up to **Skiddaw House Hostel**. Turn

**L** immediately in front of the building and drop to a bridge.

**7.** Cross then keep **SA**, now on semi-techie singletrack. Continue for over 5km and it eventually becomes a broad track that follows the **River Caldew** to the head of a tarmac road. Keep ahead to the T-junction in **Mosedale** and bear **R** to the bridge.

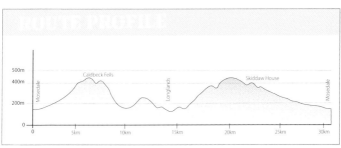

**Start/Finish:** Mosedale Bridge

**Grid ref:** NY 357 322; **Approx postcode:** CA11 0XG

**Nearest town:** Keswick

**Total distance:** 32km/20 miles

**Total ascent:** 950m

**Approx time:** 3-4 hrs

**OS Map:** OL4 & OL 5 *The English Lakes North-western & North-eastern Areas*

**Refreshments:** None on route; plenty in **Keswick** if you divert.

**Best time:** Most of the trails are firm and will work all year round, but the singletrack from **Skiddaw House** back to **Mosedale** at the end gets a bit boggy in places.

**Want more:** Link it with **Lonscale Fell (Route 22)** to make a Hard option.

**Weekend away:** With **Keswick** as a base, you're in easy reach of **Route 20** and **Route 22**, and you're not so far from **16, 17** & **18** either—that's a week's worth.

# LONSCALE FELL

**Easy** 2/3 hrs

↑ 600m

**TOP FIVE**

*Technical singletrack on the flanks of Lonscale Fell*

**UNDULATING** **TECHNICAL** **SINGLETRACK** **BAD WEATHER**

**EASY**

## IN BRIEF

If all 'natural' trails were like these there'd be no trail centres. At just 17km it's an easy jaunt by anyone's standards. And a fit and competent mountain biker could knock it off in less than 2 hours. But this loop is also one of the best going, with a couple of full-on techie sections that will challenge even the best. The climb from **Glenderaterra Beck** sets the tone: it can definitely be done, but only if you get it 100% right—no mean feat. And the steep singletrack onto the flanks of **Lonscale Fell** ups the ante another notch. But the real fun comes on the slick rock terrace sliced into **Lonscale Crags**. It looks do-able; but that's a hell of a long way to fall if you get it wrong. And if you foot the first time, do you have the nerve for another go? It's plain sailing from there on—and mainly downhill too.

# LONSCALE FELL

**Lonscale Fell** is the lower of the two lofty tops that make up the south east ridge of the mighty **Skiddaw**—see extension suggestion. It's a bulky, grassy mound really, with little true definition; but the trail gouged into its eastern and southern flanks cuts a precarious line and makes a fine crux to a short but very sweet outing.

## THE ROUTE   Start: **Threlkeld** car park (GR: NY 318 256)

**START**   Turn **R** out of the car park onto the lane and climb easily up past the **Blencathra Visitor Centre** and out onto the fellside. Stay on this main track, rising and dropping several times until you finally drop to a bridge over **Glenderaterra Beck**.

**2.** Cross this and stay on the main trail to climb up the opposite hillside, along the side of a wall. Ignore a **L** fork and continue on the main track until it T's into

*Cruisy going above Latrigg*

another track at the top. Turn **L** onto this and follow it for over 4km, around **Lonscale Crag**, where it gets very technical, and then down into **Whit Beck**. Continue easily around the hillside to the car park at Latrigg.

(**Skiddaw Extension**: Climb away from **Whit Beck** and then continue around the hillside to a gate and obvious path leading sharp **R**. Take this and clamber over **Low Man** to the summit. Return by the same route)

**3.** Turn right into the car park. Turn **L**, through a gate, at the far end, and follow the bridleway down, keeping **R** at a fork after 1km. This drops steeply through woodland (beware—it's popular with walkers) and eventually crosses the **A66** and continues to a road.

**4.** Turn **L** and keep **R** at a fork to continue to a roundabout, by the old station buildings. Head into the car park and keep the buildings to your **R** to join the old railway line, which you now follow for 4km. This ends alongside the A66. Turn **L** towards **Threlkeld**, and then fork **L**, in the village, to climb back up to the car park.

*Dry trails beneath Lonscale Fell*

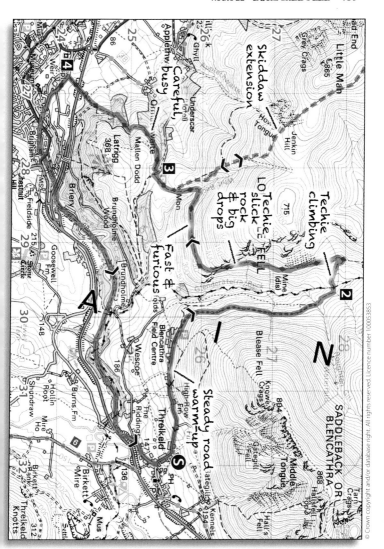

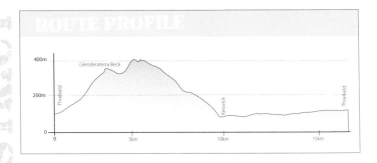

## ROUTE PROFILE

400m — Glenderaterra Beck

200m — Threlkeld — Keswick — Threlkeld

0 — 0 — 5km — 10km — 15km

## NEED TO KNOW

**Start/Finish:** Threlkeld car park

**Grid ref:** NY 318 256; **Approx postcode:** CA12 4SB

**Nearest town:** Keswick

**Total distance:** 17km/11 miles

**Total ascent:** 600m

**Approx time:** 2-3 hrs

**OS Map:** OL4 & OL 5 *The English Lakes North-western & North-eastern Areas*

**Refreshments:** None on route; plenty in **Keswick** if you divert.

**Best time:** Great trails that drain well and will work all year round. Best to avoid busy weekends though as the path from **Keswick** to **Latrigg** is extremely busy.

**Want more:** Link with **Route 21** for a Hard tour of the area, or tackle the **Skiddaw Extension** as described in the route description.

**Weekend way:** With **Keswick** as a base, you're in easy reach of **Route 20** and **Route 21**, and not so far from **16, 17** &**18**. That's a week's worth.

# GHOST

# The FuturE:is Now

For the first time, your rear suspension adjusts automatically to all riding conditions. Propulsion, traction and comfort no longer compete with each other. Now your bicycle provides all you need without any compromise.

## BOTTOM BRACKET SENSOR
Senses crank rotation and transmits status to the computer.

## FORK SENSORS
Two sensors determine the perfect E:i Shock position by measuring fork acceleration.

## INTELLIGENT COMPUTER
Computes all data and transmits the perfect settings to the E:i Shock.

## POWERFUL BATTERY
A powerful battery provides the energy for long-lasting riding fun.

## MULTI-FUNCTIONAL DISPLAY
The display combines functions of a high-quality tachometer with the status display of the E:i Shock system.

## AUTOMATIC SHOCK ADJUSTMENT
The EI shock system automatically adapts to terrain and rider input adjusting your suspension settings as quickly as every 0.1 seconds. This ensures that you are always in the optimum setting and getting ultimate performance from your suspension.

Multi-information Display

Automatic Shock Adjustment

Powerful Battery

Fork Sensor

Bottom Bracket Sensor

# APPENDIXES

## BIKE SHOPS

**Arragon's**, Penrith 01768 890344
**Askew Cycles**, Kendal 01539 728057
**Biketreks**, Ambleside 01539 431245
**Cyclewise**, Whinlatter Forest 01768 778711*
**Evans**, Kendal 01539 7400876
**Gill Cycles**, Ulverston 01229 581116
**Ghyllside Cycles**, Ambleside 01539 433592
**Grizedale Mountain Bikes**, Grizedale 01229 860335*
**Keswick Mountain Bikes** (main shop), Keswick 01768 780586* (workshop), Keswick 01768 774407
**Wheelbase**, Staveley 01539 821443*
**Whinlatter Bikes**, Keswick 01768 773940
* Hire available

## TOURIST INFORMATION

**Ambleside TIC** 01539 432582
**Bowness TIC** 01539 442895
**Carlisle TIC** 01228 625600
**Cockermouth TIC** 01900 822634
**Coniston TIC** 01539 441533
**Hawkshead TIC** 01539 436946
**Kendal TIC** 01539 797516
**Keswick TIC** 01768 772645
**Penrith TIC** 01768 867466
**Sedbergh TIC** 01539 620125
**Ullswater TIC** 01768 482414
www.lakedistrict.gov.uk
www.golakes.co.uk

## RECOMMENDED PUBS

**Britannia Inn**, Elterwater 01539 437210
**Church House Inn**, Torver 01539 441282
**Mill Inn**, Mungrisdale 01768 79632
**Newfield Inn**, Seathwaite 01229 716208
**Old Dungeon Ghyll Hotel**, Great Langdale 01539 437272

**Watermill Inn**, Ings 01539 821309
**Woolpack Inn**, Boot 01946 433363

## RECOMMENDED CAFÉS

**Wilf's**, Staveley 01539 822329
**Café Treff,** Ambleside 01539 431027
**The Lakeland Pedlar**, Keswick 01768 774492

## RECOMMENDED B&B

**Britannia Inn**, Elterwater 01539 437210
**Beech House**, Kendal 01539 720385
**Beech House**, Glenridding 01768 482037
**Church House Inn**, Torver 01539 441282
**Mill Inn**, Mungrisdale 01768 79632
**Watermill Inn**, Ings 01539 821309
**Woolpack Inn**, Boot 01946 433363

## YOUTH HOSTELS

**Alston**, 01434 381509
**Ambleside**, 0845 371 9620
**Arnside**, 0845 371 9722
**Longthwaite**, 0845 371 9624
**Buttermere**, 0845 371 9508
**Caldbeck Bunkhouse**, 01768 812280
**Cockermouth**, 0845 371 9313
**Coniston Coppermines**, 0845 371 9630
**Coniston Holly How**, 0845 371 9511
**Elterwater**, 0845 371 9017
**Ennerdale**, 0845 371 9116
**Eskdale**, 0845 371 9317
**Grasmere**, 0845 371 9319
**Hawkshead**, 0845 371 9321
**Hawse End Bunkhouse**, 01768 812280
**Glenridding**, 0845 371 9742
**Seatoller,** 0845 371 9522
**Keswick**, 0845 371 9746
**High Close**, 0845 371 9748
**Patterdale**, 0845 371 9337
**Wasdale**, 0845 371 9350
**Troutbeck**, 0845 371 9352

# WEATHER INFORMATION

The weather in the Lakeland Fells is incredibly fickle and many a good day out is ruined by choosing the wrong route for the conditions. In extreme cases, poor weather can be dangerous—it's scary how quickly you can get cold on a summit even in summer.

It's always best to check the weather when you do your initial planning and then again on the morning of the ride. The easiest and cheapest way to do this is via the internet using one or more of the sites listed below but it is also possible to check via local radio or TV or many hotels will actually post a daily weather update.

If all else fails, the nearest TIC should be able to advise

Weather Websites

www.mwis.org.uk

www.metoffice.gov.uk/loutdoor/mountainsafety

## Telephone Weather Services

Weatherline tel 0844 846 2444

## Mountain Rescue by SMS Text

It is now possible to alert the emergency services by SMS text—extremely useful if you have a low battery or intermittent signal. But in order to do this, you do need to register your phone first. To register, simply text "register" to 999 and then follow the instructions in the reply. Do it now—it could save yours or someone else's life.

www.emergencysms.org.uk